ENVIRONMENTAL REGULATION
and the
U.S. ECONOMY

ENVIRONMENTAL REGULATION
and the
U.S. ECONOMY

Edited by Henry M. Peskin, Paul R. Portney,
and Allen V. Kneese

With contributions by
Barry P. Bosworth
Gregory B. Christainsen
Winston Harrington
Robert H. Haveman
Alan J. Krupnick
Ronald G. Ridker
William D. Watson

*Published for Resources for the Future
By The Johns Hopkins University Press
Baltimore and London*

This book is reprinted with permission from the
Natural Resources Journal, Vol. 21, No. 3, July 1981.

Published for Resources for the Future
By The Johns Hopkins University Press,
Baltimore, Maryland 21218

Library of Congress Catalog Card No. 81-47620

ISBN 0-8018-2711-6 hardcover
      0-8018-2712-4 paperback

RESOURCES FOR THE FUTURE, INC.
1755 Massachusetts Avenue, N.W., Washington, D.C. 20036

Resources for the Future is a nonprofit organization for research and education in the development, conservation, and use of natural resources and the improvement of the quality of the environment. It was established in 1952 with the cooperation of the Ford Foundation. Grants for research are accepted from government and private sources only on the condition that RFF shall be solely responsible for the conduct of the research and free to make its results available to the public. Most of the work of Resources for the Future is carried out by its resident staff; part is supported by grants to universities and other nonprofit organizations. Unless otherwise stated, interpretations and conclusions in RFF publications are those of the authors; the organization takes responsibility for the selection of significant subjects for study, the competence of the researchers, and their freedom of inquiry.

This work was prepared in RFF's Quality of the Environment Division, Clifford S. Russell, director. It was edited by Ruth B. Haas.

Contents

Contents

Preface and Acknowledgments

Resources for the Future has long been interested not only in the design of environmental policies but also in the effects of those policies when they are implemented. Among the most important of these are the effects of environmental regulation on the health of the U.S. economy. Accordingly, during the summer and fall of 1980, Henry M. Peskin, Paul R. Portney, and Allen V. Kneese began to pull together work being done by researchers at RFF and elsewhere that bears on the macroeconomic effects of environmental regulations in the United States. This volume represents the individual and collective judgments of these researchers about some of the most important and hotly debated effects of environmental regulation.

The editors are grateful to Christopher Caton, Robert Crandall, Joy Hecht, Robert Leone, and Clifford Russell for their comments on earlier versions of some or all of the papers in this volume, as well as to Edith Brashares, who provided valuable research assistance. Ruth Haas also provided valuable assistance in the preparation of the manuscript. Eileen LesCallett, Mae Barnes, Martha Bari, and Margaret Parr-Recard typed the manuscript. Their efforts were coordinated by Joy Hecht.

The editors also wish to acknowledge the financial support they have received during the preparation of this volume from the Andrew W. Mellon Foundation, the Environmental Assessment Council of the Academy of Natural Sciences, the Council on Environmental Quality, and the Esther A. and Joseph Klingenstein Fund, Inc.

These papers have been published separately in the July 1981 issue of the *Natural Resources Journal.*

H. M. P.
P. R. P.
July 1981
A. V. K.

Introduction

HENRY M. PESKIN, PAUL R. PORTNEY, and ALLEN V. KNEESE

Along with many other developed nations, the United States is currently experiencing economic difficulties that many feel are unprecedented. The common symptoms appear to be a substantial decline in the rate of growth of real income and productivity, increasing numbers of unemployed, and inflation rates that seem to be immune to conventional therapies. Under such bleak circumstances, it is only natural to expect that any and all possible causes of difficulties will be closely scrutinized. A currently popular candidate for scrutiny is governmental regulation in general and environmental regulation in particular.

If, in fact, environmental regulations are an important contributor to our current economic difficulties, it may be because the costs of those regulations were ignored or underestimated when the legislation was passed. There might exist, as a consequence, a bias toward too much regulation. Yet, even if environmental regulations are not a cause of our economic difficulties, the public may perceive them to be so. This perception—the feeling that there is too much regulation—and the belt-tightening that can be expected as a result of slow growth and inflation, is already beginning to spell trouble for environmental regulation.

This set of papers explores the relationship between federal environmental regulation and the performance of the U.S. economy. This subject is clearly large and encompasses many issues. We wish to emphasize at the outset that certain important issues in environmental regulation are not covered in this volume. Since the primary concern of these papers is aggregate economic activity, there is only incidental mention of the effect that environmental policies may have on specific industries, plants, firms, individuals, and geographic regions. Perhaps more important, there is very little mention of the benefits of environmental regulation. This is because these benefits generally do not show up in the national income accounts, and hence are unlikely to influence significantly the rates of inflation, unemployment, and other macroeconomic indicators that are used to judge the health of the economy. (In fact, this is the subject of one of the papers.) The lack of attention to benefits should not, therefore, be taken to imply that we or the authors of the papers consider them to be insignificant: indeed, these benefits are probably quite large.

This absence of cost-benefit comparisons, as well as any mention of the distributional implications of environmental regulation, means

1

that there is simply not enough material in these papers for one to draw a sweeping conclusion about the overall desirability of our environmental policies. Instead, the authors concentrate primarily on the macroeconomic impacts of regulation. Needless to say, we think this is a very significant aspect.

While the rest of the papers in this volume discuss some aspect of the effect of environmental regulation on the economy, Barry Bosworth's paper is unique: it considers the effect of future macroeconomic conditions on environmental and other regulations. He discusses three major U.S. economic concerns—the high inflation rate, the recent and substantial reduction in the rate of productivity growth, and the erosion of the international competitive position of U.S. industry. These problems, which Bosworth feels are likely to remain serious in the 1980s, will affect the way existing and proposed regulations are viewed during the period.

For example, Bosworth suggests that if anti-inflationary policies force workers to accept unemployment or falling real incomes, they may be suspicious of or hostile toward environmental policies that increase prices. Furthermore, according to Bosworth, reduced productivity growth will make it difficult to garner support for new environmental regulations if these regulations imply that some groups will gain at the expense of others. In the past, productivity increases made it possible to initiate new social programs at the same time incomes were increasing. Those groups that would have lost in a static economy were often compensated by increased growth. Finally, Bosworth identifies two industries, steel and automobiles, where wages are much higher than elsewhere in the manufacturing sector. Although he suggests that these wage concessions are responsible for much of their problems with import competition, Bosworth points out that both industries have blamed regulation for their difficulties. Future problems in these and other industries may lead to pressure for reductions in their regulatory burden.

One implication of Bosworth's observations is that it would be well for environmental regulators to hasten their search for the most cost-effective policies possible. Carefully designed policies will make fewer demands on what appears to be a limited and slowly growing stock of national economic resources. In addition, such policies will appear less intrusive and thus more politically acceptable.

Increased public awareness of the benefits of environmental policies may help alleviate some of the economic dislocations associated with these policies. As Bosworth notes, when some workers maintain real incomes in the face of price increases caused by environmental regulations, they are actually receiving "double compensation." For, as he argues, if workers successfully negotiate wage bargains to compensate them for all price increases, not only will they have constant real wages, but also the advantages of a clean environment. Their wage increases trigger higher prices and higher wage demands from others; this perpetuates the cost-push cycle. Workers can be expected to push for wage increases even when regulation confers nonmonetary gains upon them. But a better knowledge of environmental benefits may give employers and the government something to point to in attempting to resist these demands. This may help alleviate the pressure for double compensation.

Even those who believe that environmental regulation is a major source of our economic woes recognize that many other factors influence economic performance. One way to gauge the relative contribution of each of these is to use models to mathematically describe their interactions. Since such models are an important means for obtaining a reasonably objective and comprehensive analysis of the macroeconomic effects of environmental regulations, Paul Portney discusses the better known models in some detail.

Besides describing the methodologies, limitations, and results of several studies, Portney also discusses what is known about pollution control expenditures. These are the most important data that go into the macroeconomic studies. While expenditure estimates are widely quoted and essential for the modeling studies, they are poorly understood, even by those who use them freely. As Portney points out, pollution control expenditures are not the same as the social costs of regulation, even though the terms often are used interchangeably. Moreover, the methods and sources for estimating these data differ substantially among different investigators and, yet, these methods and data sources are usually unknown to those who use the estimates.

For these reasons and several others Portney discusses, the general conclusion drawn from the macroeconomic modeling studies—that environmental regulations have a rather small effect on economic activity—should be viewed with some caution. There are weaknesses in both the data and the models that are used. Indeed, it will be some time before these models are developed to a point where they can adequately treat all the factors that affect the economy and which are affected by environmental regulation.

While Portney's paper discusses large models that describe many indicators of economic activity, the next two papers concentrate on two of these indicators: productivity and the gross national product. Robert Haveman and Gregory Christainsen explore recent declines in the growth rate of U.S. productivity, which is of special concern for two reasons: first, because of its implications for economic growth and inflation; and second because the public associates this decline with a general decline in America's perceived leadership in economic production, product quality, workmanship, and innovation. As a result, for perhaps the first time in U.S. history, polls indicate that many Americans feel that their children may end up worse off than themselves.

Haveman and Christainsen discuss the possible links between regulation and productivity. They point out that there are many other factors—the energy crisis, changes in the age-sex composition of the labor force, and shifts in the composition of production from manufacturing to services, to name just a few—that also could contribute to productivity declines. Indeed, after reviewing the available estimates of the relationship between regulation and productivity, they conclude that only a small fraction, perhaps 8 to 12 percent, of the recent decline should be attributed to environmental regulation.

They caution, however, that empirical analyses are unable to account for certain possibly adverse effects that may be associated with regulatory delay, paper work, and uncertainty about future requirements.

On the other hand, the productivity measures Haveman and Christainsen consider are limited in an important respect: the "output" upon which their calculation is based includes only those items measured in the national income accounts. Since these accounts in general do *not* include changes in environmental quality, productivity may fall even if very little in the way of conventional output has been traded for substantial increases in environmental output.

The best-known measure of conventional economic output is the gross national product (GNP). For this reason, Henry Peskin's paper looks closely at this indicator. In particular, Peskin investigates to what extent conventional GNP already appropriately measures changes in the quality of the environment; whether it is feasible to modify GNP to more accurately reflect environmental change; and, if feasible, whether such modifications are desirable.

In spite of its wide use as an indicator of economic output, GNP is nevertheless a very limited measure of economic well-being. It ignores altogether the composition of output and its distribution among the population. Furthermore, even though national income accounting focuses on production, productive activity that takes place outside of the marketplace—in the household, for example—is also ignored. It is not surprising that GNP is a poor indicator of changes in environmental quality.

Peskin also discusses U.S. and Japanese proposals to modify the GNP to make it a better indicator of well-being. While none of the proposed measures is free of deficiencies, and although all pose problems to those wishing to implement changes, Peskin recommends that these efforts be explored further. He suggests, however, that they proceed parallel to, but not as a substitute for, the existing effort to measure conventional GNP. A governmental attempt to measure alternative versions of GNP would signal the public that although conventional GNP is a useful measure, the government recognizes its deficiencies as a measure of well-being.

While there may be some question about their quantitative importance, several of the papers suggest that environmental regulations will have adverse effects on at least some measures of economic activity. Yet, as Winston Harrington and Alan Krupnick point out in their paper, many of these adverse effects can be moderated by changes in the way the country goes about regulating.

Currently, environmental policy relies to a large extent on the promulgation of technology-based regulations. Harrington and Krupnick briefly review the legislation supporting this approach, with special emphasis on the 1977 amendments to the Clean Air and Clean Water acts. Because of complexities and uncertainties associated with their implementation, these amendments have the potential for generating more severe economic effects than have been observed in the past.

Harrington and Krupnick consider several possible alterations in regulatory procedures. Some of these, referred to as "procedural reforms," could be implemented with little or no change in existing legislation. These reforms, some of which are already under way, include a number of technical changes in rulemaking procedures (for example, using EPA contractors differently and classifying industries differently), changed permit procedures (for example, longer permit life), use of standards based on cost-effectiveness, and permission for waivers for those firms which will develop innovative, less costly pollution control methods.

Other approaches, referred to as "substantive reforms," represent more of a break with the current regulatory approach. These approaches include EPA's new bubble policy and related offset policies, the use of marketable pollution permits, and effluent charges.

Such economic incentives have long been advocated by economists because of the cost savings they might make possible. In addition to the cost-saving properties of incentive-based regulation, Harrington and Krupnick point to another reason for using this approach. Not only does it have desirable efficiency properties, it also appears to interfere less with the functioning of the economy than the present regulatory approach.

Up to and including Peskin's paper, all the authors take a rather short-term view of the relationship between environmental regulation and economic activity. Their concern is with existing regulations and recent economic conditions. However, it is also important to understand as best we can the long-run relationship between environmental policy and economic conditions.

In their paper Ronald Ridker and William Watson provide a methodology for taking the longer view. Using an input-output model, some illustrative data, and some assumptions about population growth and technological change, they simulate the effects of several hypothetical environmental policies well into the next century. Their model attempts to account for the pressures that increased population and economic growth exert on fixed amounts of available environmental resources, as well as the effects of technological progress. Economic and population growth tends to increase the benefits that may obtain from environmental regulation, while technological progress tends to decrease the costs of these regulations.

Thus, the Ridker–Watson paper shows that conclusions drawn from the near term may change once one takes a longer view. In particular, environmental policies that may appear too costly from today's perspective *may* appear socially and economically desirable once their long-term consequences are accounted for. However, as the authors are quick to point out, one must treat the conclusions from such a long-run analysis even more carefully than those obtained from short-term models.

The 1970s have aptly been called "the environmental decade" because of the large body of environmental legislation that was put in place during that time by the Congress. But the implementation of that legislation is still going on and will last well into the 1980s. The legislation will undergo its full test during a decade that threatens to present us with many economic difficulties. It is therefore more important than ever before to try to understand the forces that bear on macroeconomic performance. The papers in this volume should add to an understanding of the influence of environmental regulation.

The Economic Environment for Regulation in the 1980s

BARRY P. BOSWORTH*

In recent years substantial criticism has been directed at government regulatory activities across a broad range of areas because they are perceived as contributing to the worsening economic position of the United States. While the effects of regulation on the economy constitute the primary subject of this volume, it is also true that general economic conditions help shape the environment of opinion in which new regulations are prepared and old ones revised or eliminated. This paper identifies several factors that are likely to affect the economy in the decade to come, and discusses their implications for environmental regulation.

After a decade of strong expansion in the 1960s, economic growth came to be taken for granted; attention was increasingly directed toward managing an affluent society. Emphasis in public policy shifted to such matters as improving the distribution of income, and protecting consumers, workers and the environment from the external costs of an industrial society. These issues, while important in their own right, obtained a high degree of public support because of the perception that the general goal of economic growth could be achieved on a sustained basis. In addition, the potential competition with other claims on the nation's economic resources was minimized because the focus of the discussion was directed toward how to spend the growth dividend of future years.[1]

The pendulum began to swing back toward a greater emphasis on prices and output during the 1970s. Worsening difficulties with inflation and stagnant or falling real incomes increased public concern with the state of the economy and motivated an intensive search for villains. As in any period of dissatisfaction, the activities of government, including fiscal, regulatory, and administrative activities, provide a highly visible focal point for such discontent.

As we enter the 1980s, the issues of inflation, employment, and economic growth have reemerged as the central concerns of eco-

---

*Barry Bosworth is a senior fellow in the Economic Studies Division of the Brookings Institution.

1. In some cases the proponents of these programs denied the existence of a conflict with other resource claims. It was argued that these demands would generate their own supply and further the expansion of the nation's material wealth.

nomic policy. Inflation is in excess of 10 percent on a sustained basis, unemployment is above the critical levels that triggered the expansionary policies of the early 1960s, productivity growth has fallen to about a third of its historical trend, industrial capacity is inadequate to employ the expanded work force of the 1970s, and the economy is extremely vulnerable to disruptions in world energy and food markets. All of this suggests that the 1980s will be dominated by severe constraints in every area and increased social and economic conflict. In sum, the coming decade will not be conducive to the expansion of programs limiting the external costs of industrial growth.

There is a growing professional consensus and public understanding that the economic problems we face in the 1980s are serious. However, there is no similar consensus with respect to the policy actions that should be taken in response. In part, this lack of consensus reflects the fact that policies best suited to deal with each problem in isolation conflict with those required in other areas. There is fairly widespread agreement, for example, that a sustained period of demand restraint is a necessary ingredient of an effective anti-inflation policy. Yet, such restraint and slow growth is not conducive to the increased capital formation necessary to increase productivity growth and expand industrial capacity. Disputes also arise because different policies impose burdens and sacrifice on different groups.

The general theme of this paper—that the 1980s must be seen as a decade of severe constraints on economic gains and policies—can be highlighted by focusing on three issues: inflation, productivity growth, and the competitive position of major U.S. industries. The first two are of concern for environmental regulation because they suggest a heightened degree of competition for scarce resources. The third is important because those industries subject to the most severe competitive problems in world markets are often affected significantly by government regulations. In the search for measures by which government can assist in the "revitalization" of these industries, it is only natural that a reduction of regulation will be high on their agenda—even if regulatory costs are not a significant cause of their problems.

INFLATION

Current inflation can be most aptly described as a combination of two factors. First, there exists a self-perpetuating underlying cycle of wage and price inflation that is only loosely related to overall demand conditions; it is more reflective of past inflation and expectations of future inflation. Second, our current inflation is affected by a series of shocks or disturbances that exacerbate the underlying rate, raising it to a higher plateau.

The high underlying rate of inflation occurs because each individual perceives his own actions as a defensive response to the inflationary actions of others. Wage demands are fueled, not by a perception of labor shortages, but by a desire to match past price increases and the wages of others and by expectations that the process will continue. On the price side, most business firms justify their price increases as a simple pass-through of higher costs. That is, everyone participates in perpetuating inflation, but no one sees himself as the cause. While most persons realize that they are not gaining from this repetitive cycle, no one dares to exercise restraint because there is no assurance that others will do the same. Indeed, it is a variant of the now-familiar "prisoner's dilemma" in which we are all prisoners of inflation.[2]

In the past decade, the United States has also experienced an unusual number of shocks that have exacerbated price inflation and raised it to new heights. This has happened because the increased integration of the world economy leaves the United States far more vulnerable to crop failures, sharp increases in petroleum prices, or other disruptions in international markets. Large price increases in these markets can have an immediate dramatic impact on the inflation rate, but the effects become longer lasting when everyone else escalates their wage and price increases in an effort to catch up. The result is an upward ratcheting of the underlying rate and a carryover of inflation into future years.

The underlying momentum of industrial wage and price increases has, for several years, averaged 7 to 8 percent annually.[3] But in 1978–79, sharp price increases for food, housing, and energy drove the overall inflation rate to an annual rate of 13 percent.[4] In early 1980, sharply higher interest rates temporarily raised the rate of increase of the consumer price index as high as 18 percent on an annual basis.[5] While the worst of these shocks may be behind us, the effort to catch up with this last burst of price increases is leading to a steady escalation of domestic wage and price increases and an upward ratcheting of inflationary momentum. Thus, the United States enters the 1980s

---

2. The term "prisoner's dilemma" derived from the problem faced by two prisoners, who are interrogated separately. If one accuses the other, he may go free, unless he himself is accused. Thus, acting individually, they will choose a strategy inferior to that which would emerge if they acted together to deny any wrongdoing.

3. Bosworth, *Economic Policy*, in SETTING NATIONAL PRIORITIES: AGENDA FOR THE 1980s, at 43 (J. Pechman ed. 1981).

4. ECONOMIC REPORT OF THE PRESIDENT (1981).

5. *Id.*

with a built-in and self-sustaining inflation rate of about 10 percent and a continuing vulnerability to further shocks that could drive inflation far higher.

The tasks for economic policy, therefore, are twofold: breaking the momentum of the underlying wage-price cycle, and finding a means of avoiding or dampening the influence of potential future shocks that threaten to accelerate the process. The resulting dilemma is that the effort to break the momentum of the wage-price cycle with the traditional tools of fiscal and monetary restraint can be successful only at the cost of high levels of unemployment for a sustained period. At the same time, little or nothing has been done to reduce the vulnerability of the economy to the types of inflationary shocks that proved costly in the 1970s.

Inflation has often been described as a purely monetary phenomenon. In fact, there is substantial truth to the argument that if the growth of the money supply (adjusted for secular trends in velocity) does not exceed the growth in physical output, inflation cannot continue for long. At the same time, the supply of money is controlled by government. Thus, from one perspective, inflation can be viewed as a political rather than an economic problem.

The term "monetary restraint," however, should be understood as a euphemism for a process by which a refusal to increase the money supply in the face of inflation raises interest rates, reduces demand, and lowers output and employment. Increased competition for jobs and sales forces restraint in wages and prices. In effect, control over the money supply is the means by which a society forces a reconciliation of the demand for more with the constraint of that which is available. By controlling the pool of the unemployed, government can control inflation.

The difficulties for anti-inflation policy emerge from the application of this model to the real world. In many markets, prices and wages appear to be highly insensitive to variations in demand. Instead, the major effect of a reduction in demand is a reduction in production and employment, without the expected larger effect on prices and wages. Thus, the refusal of the monetary authorities to accommodate inflation requires the explicit acceptance of increased unemployment and lost output. This same problem is equally evident with respect to inflationary shocks. In theory, a rise in food or energy prices should change relative prices but not the average price level. Increased expenditures on products whose prices have risen implies reduced demands for other products and should make for offsetting declines in other prices. Yet, reduced demand for products such as automobiles in response to higher energy prices is likely to result in offsetting reductions in production rather than prices. In the face of this conflict, monetary authorities have normally opted for a compromise of partial accommodation with some rise in inflation and some increase in unemployment—a situation which has satisfied no one.

Much of the recent discussion of anti-inflation policy has emphasized a gradualist approach, whereby a high but not extreme level of unemployment and slow growth is tolerated over a period of several years. Even the most optimistic estimates, however, suggest that such a policy would require nearly a decade of very slow growth in aggregate demand to have an appreciable effect on the inflation rate. There are doubts that the political process could stand the strain, and the gradualist approach may set in motion strong pressures by individual interest groups to achieve changes in the rules and institutions (e.g., trade protection and minimum price and wage laws) to protect themselves against the consequences of such a policy—thus intensifying the basic problem. Such a policy is also highly vulnerable to disruptive shocks, similar to those of the 1970s, that would negate any of the gains.

The alternative of extreme fiscal and monetary restraint offers the opportunity for greater immediate gains against inflation, but the pressures for a reversal of the policies in the face of sharply higher unemployment would be strong. In effect, this is the program being pursued in Great Britain, where the government has followed a policy of severe restraint combined with repeated emphasis that it will not back down in its refusal to accommodate continued inflation. While the outcome of that policy remains in doubt, the risks of the policy—both political and economic—are substantial since it polarizes public views. While economists in the United States continue to debate the precise magnitude of the unemployment costs, public opinion about demand restraint is likely to reflect individuals' perceptions of whether or not they will lose their own jobs.

On the other hand, there are substantial problems with anti-inflation policies that do not emphasize demand restraint. The failure to contain inflation in 1979–80 has done much to destroy the credibility of voluntary restraint programs. There is scant belief that restraint in one's own wage and price demands will be matched by similar efforts by others, while the difficulties of 1973–74 have convinced many economists and policymakers that wage and price controls are ineffective. Whether voluntary or mandatory, such programs are particularly difficult to operate in a world of sharply changing relative prices when a single rule cannot apply to all markets; they are ineffective in the face of shortages; and they attract the strong opposition of those interest groups who feel that they would be disadvantaged.

Finally, the insensitivity of some wages and prices to competitive pressures has led some economists to advocate the uses of tax-based incentive policies (TIPs) to encourage adherence to a wage-price guideline.[6] On a sustained basis, any such program would require both a penalty for excessive increases as well as a credit for compliance if the tax credit is not to erode tax revenues. However, defining and monitoring compliance under a TIP program raises problems of wage and price measurement that are equal to those of a full-blown controls program. The administrative problems of measuring compliance may be less bothersome for a temporary program. Yet, a tax incentive program of a size sufficient to have a dramatic short-run effect would severely strain budgeting resources. As such, it would compete with other proposals to use future tax cuts to promote capital formation.

In light of the difficulties with other approaches, it is likely that demand restraint will continue to be the focal point for anti-inflation policies. This seems particularly evident in the increased emphasis in recent years on the need for restricting monetary growth rates. Within this framework, it is extremely unlikely that monetary policy will accommodate any significant recovery of economic activity as long as inflation continues to run in the neighborhood of 10 percent. While efforts may be made to adopt a more stimulative fiscal policy through tax cuts, the principal result is likely to be higher interest rates, rather than increased growth.

This effect has an important implication for environmental and other regulation in the years to come. If unemployment and forgone real output are being tolerated to fight inflation, government or other policies that serve to increase prices will be viewed suspiciously. Since regulatory policies have this effect,[7] they will come under careful review and may be opposed by those who are suffering in the name of demand restraint. In other words, those who are under- or unemployed because of demand restraint may see the relaxation of regulation as a "better" way to fight inflation.

This will be true even when regulation is well founded and forces firms to bear costs they have heretofore imposed on others. Similarly, attempts to remove subsidies to energy users or others benefitting from suboptimally low prices may be opposed on grounds of infla-

---

6. CURING CHRONIC INFLATION (A. Okun & G. Perry eds. 1978).
7. *See* Portney's paper in this volume.

tion. Thus, even policies which pass rigorous cost-benefit tests will have tough sledding in an anti-inflationary period.

Note that the "catch-up" phenomenon discussed above will amplify any direct effect of regulation on prices. When the higher costs associated with regulation are passed on in higher prices, wage earners will try to maintain purchasing power by demanding higher wages. They will do this even though they are already being "compensated" for higher prices by the improvements in environmental quality resulting from the regulation. In effect, by demanding higher wages to offset regulation-induced price increases, workers are requesting double compensation. When their wage demands are rewarded, it serves to perpetuate and increase the underlying inflation rate.

It is difficult to determine the precise size of "the catch-up" relative to an initial increase in price caused by regulation or some other change in policy. On average, however, the existing empirical models suggest that the effect is to double the impact on the price level within a two-year period.[8] Thus, an initial set of government actions that raise the price level by 1 percent will ultimately lead to a 2 percent rise in prices. If the monetary authorities refuse to accommodate these price pressures by increasing the money supply, the same models suggest that unemployment would need to rise by about 1 percent. Individual regulatory and other administrative actions of government tend to have a small effect on the price level, but the cumulative impact of such measures can be substantial.

REAL INCOMES AND PRODUCTIVITY GROWTH

Much of the increased public concern with inflation in recent years has been the result of a dramatic surge in price inflation that has not been matched by an acceleration of wage increases. Yet, inflation alone does not explain the failure of average wage gains to match the increase in the price level. Other factors are of major importance. In particular, the decline in real wages highlights a problem that has attracted less attention than inflation—the sharp slowdown in productivity growth. The following data illustrate the effect of diminished productivity growth.

Real Wage Trends

The slowing of real wage growth for workers in the nonfarm business sector of the economy is evident in the data of Table 1. Despite an increase in the rate of growth of nominal wages from 4.5 percent

---

8. Author's unpublished estimate derived from simulations of the FRB-MIT-PENN econometric model.

TABLE 1

TRENDS IN NOMINAL AND REAL WAGE RATES
(annual percentage rates of change, adjusted for inflation)

	Annual percentage change		
	1959–69	1969–79	1978–79
Nominal wage rate	4.5	7.3	7.8
Consumer prices (CPI)	2.3	7.1	11.3
Real-wage rate	2.1	0.2	−3.1
Contribution to real wages of change in:			
Productivity	2.2	1.1	−2.2
Wage share	0.5	0.4	1.8
Employer taxes	−0.1	−0.2	−0.2
Nonwage benefits	−0.1	−0.5	−0.3
Prices paid-vs.-received	−0.2	−0.6	−2.3
Addenda:			
Influence of alternative measure of consumer prices			
CPI minus consumer expenditure deflator	0.0	0.7	2.2

Source: Author's calculations and unpublished data on compensation and productivity from the Bureau of Labor Statistics, U.S. Department of Labor, and the Bureau of Economic Analysis, U.S. Department of Commerce.

annually in the 1960s to 7.3 percent in the 1970s, real wage rate growth slowed from 2.1 percent to 0.2 percent per year during that period. Real wage rates actually declined by 3.1 percent in 1979. The sources of this slowdown can be identified for the private nonfarm sector of the economy and are illustrated in the table.

The bulk of the slowdown is a direct result of the sharp falloff in the growth of labor productivity. In the 1960s, the growth of labor productivity matched the growth in real wage rates—2.2 percent annually. Productivity growth began to diminish in the late 1960s, fell off to an annual average increase of 1.1 percent in the 1970s, and actually declined by 2.2 percent in 1979.[9] Thus, the slower growth of

9. Productivity improvement is central to any economy-wide expansion of real incomes. Without it, the gains of any individual or group must come at the expense of others. It also plays a crucial role in combating inflation by providing an offset to higher nominal wages and moderating the rise in unit labor costs. The causes of the productivity decline, particularly the role of environmental regulation, are discussed in Haveman's paper in this volume. Our interest here is more in its implications for real income growth and the shaping of future economic policies.

labor productivity accounted for over one half of the 1.9 percentage points of slowdown in annual real wage growth during the past decade.

On the other hand, within the private nonfarm sector, workers have gained from an increase in their share of total income. This gain comes at the expense of business (profits, interest, rent, and depreciation) and government (sales, excise, and property taxes). The change in income shares boosted the rate of growth of real wages by 0.4 percentage points annually in the 1970s compared with a 0.5 percentage point average for the prior decade. This change in the distribution of factor income is directly contrary to the commonly held view that price increases in excess of those for wages must have implied a larger profit share. Such a calculation, however, is very sensitive to business cycle fluctuations. Firms do not adjust employment fully to short-run variations in output, and these transitory changes in productivity and unit labor costs are absorbed in profit margins rather than being passed forward into prices. Thus, there is a tendency for changes in labor productivity and labor's share to offset one another over short periods. This cyclical pattern is evident in the data for 1978–79, when the impact of the productivity decline on real wages was partially offset by a sharp rise in the labor share.

Third, the rate of growth of real wages has been held down because an increasing proportion of total employment costs has been allocated to social insurance taxes and private fringe benefit programs such as pensions and medical insurance. These employer payments have increased from 8 percent of total compensation in 1959 to 16 percent in 1979. In the 1960s, the expansion of these two programs reduced the annual growth of wage rates by 0.2 percentage points. In the 1970s the differential expanded to 0.7 percentage points. While the expansion of employer payments for fringe benefits does reduce reported real-wage gains, it is quite different from the previous factors in its implication for economic welfare. Shifting the payment of health insurance from the individual to his employer, for example, lowers reported earnings but not the benefits to the worker.

Finally, the real income of workers may decline because of a loss in their "terms of trade," that is, the prices of goods they buy may rise more rapidly than the prices of the goods that they produce. Such an erosion of real incomes has occurred throughout the past two decades as prices for food, energy, and housing—important items in the consumer's budget—have risen more rapidly than the average price of the industrial products produced by American workers. Between 1978 and 1979, in particular, the more than 11 percent rise in the consumer price index (CPI) was far in excess of the 9 percent rise in the nonfarm price deflator—a 2.3 percentage point loss of real income from this effect alone.

Any conclusion about this terms-of-trade effect, however, is very dependent upon the price indexes used in the comparison. The consumer price index used to compute the increase in the cost of living is a fixed-weight index that does not allow for changes in the mix of consumer purchases from one period to the next. Thus, it overestimates the impact of higher prices on real incomes since consumers will avoid some of the higher prices by shifting the composition of their purchases. Of more importance, the CPI's conceptual treatment of some expenditure items overstates the loss of real income. The home purchase component of the index, for example, focuses on the purchase costs for new home buyers rather than the maintenance costs of existing owners. Thus, the surge of home purchase prices has a large impact on the consumer price index even though most of the real income effect is a distributional change between new and previous home owners. In addition, the financing cost component of the index moves with cyclical changes in new mortgage financing rates, even though most existing owners have fixed interest mortgages.

These conceptual issues are highlighted in the addenda to the table, which compares the effect of using the consumer price index as opposed to another index—the consumption deflator of the national income accounts—to measure real wage gains. The two indexes of consumer prices increased in parallel during the 1960s, yielding identical estimates of real wage gains; but the annual growth of real incomes in the 1970s averages 0.7 percentage points higher if the expenditures deflator is used in place of the CPI, and the difference is 2.2 percent in 1977–79. Surprisingly, therefore, a conclusion about the effect of changes in relative prices, or the terms of trade, is very dependent upon the price index chosen for such a comparison. If the consumer price index is the basis for computing consumer living costs, the terms of trade effect reduced real wage growth by 0.6 percentage points in the 1970s; but the alternative, the consumption deflator of the national income accounts, implies little or no change in terms of trade. The selection of an appropriate price index is important because many individuals receive automatic increases in their income on the basis of changes in the CPI. If the index exaggerates the inflation rate, these persons are overcompensated and the inflation problem is exacerbated.

In summary, the data of Table 1 clearly indicate that there has been a serious erosion of real wage growth over the past decade. The magnitude of that slowdown seems to be overstated by the use of the consumer price index and by the shift of income to employer-paid health and welfare plans. The decline in productivity is, however, of real consequence, and its effects on real incomes cannot be buffered indefinitely by an increase in labor's share of total income.

Real Income Trends

The notion of a slower growth in living standards is seemingly contradicted, however, by another set of data—per capita real disposable income as reported in the national income accounts. On this basis, gains in after-tax income in the 1970s nearly matched those of the prior decade. Typically, the difference between the growth of real wage rates and per capita real incomes is attributed to a growing proportion of employed persons in the total population and the use of the consumer expenditure deflator instead of the consumer price index to adjust for inflation. But trends in overall disposable income are also influenced by nonlabor incomes and changes in taxes and transfers. The influences of these various factors are illustrated in Table 2.

The table begins with *earned income* (before the deduction of employee social insurance taxes or the addition of transfer payments) per employed person in the population. All of the income measures are adjusted for inflation as measured by the consumer expenditure deflator and are expressed in per capita terms. The growth of income per employed person slowed very substantially during the 1970s,

TABLE 2

TRENDS IN PER CAPITA REAL INCOME, 1959–79
(annual rates of change, adjusted for inflation)

Total income	Annual rates of change	
	1959–69	1969–79
Earned income/employed person	2.5	0.8
Employment/population[a]	0.5	1.3
Earned income/per capita	3.1	2.2
−Employment taxes	8.7	4.3
+Transfers	5.6	6.6
Personal income	3.1	2.6
Personal taxes	5.7	2.6
Disposable income	2.7	2.5

Source: Department of Commerce, Bureau of Economic Analysis, and author's calculations.

[a]Employed persons from the household survey of the labor force.

averaging only 0.8 percent annually compared with 2.5 percent in
the 1960s. A sharp rise in the proportion of the population employed, however, did offset much of this decline in growth. The ratio
of total employment to the population rose about 2.5 times more
rapidly in the 1969–79 period than in the prior decade.[10] The effect
on *personal income* growth was also muted by a marked deceleration
of the growth in employee social insurance taxes and a rapid expansion of transfer payments, primarily social security. Thus, the decline
in the growth of per capita personal income between the two ten-year
periods was limited to 0.5 percentage points (2.6 percent annually
versus 3.1 percent). Finally, the slowdown is nearly eliminated on the
after-tax basis because personal income taxes rose at less than half
the rate of the 1960s.[11] The net result is an expansion of real disposable income at an annual rate of 2.5 percent in the 1970s compared
with 2.7 percent in the prior decade.

The upshot of all this is that the slower growth of productivity
was not fully reflected in consumer incomes during the past decade,
but these trends cannot be sustained indefinitely. The government
cannot continue to increase the share of transfer payments in the
total budget, and the budget deficit cannot again be increased to sus-
tain such payments without an offsetting rise in taxes. In fact, there
are currently strong pressures for higher defense spending, and large
increases in social insurance taxes are scheduled for the early 1980s.
Furthermore, most labor force projections suggest that the growth
rate of the employment-to-population ratio will slow in the next decade. Thus, a slow growth in productivity in future years will have a
much more evident impact on growth in real income.

Continued slow productivity growth is likely to have a major impact on economic policy during the 1980s as its implications for
growth in standard of living become more evident. It will lead to intensified conflict between different social groups. In the past, a portion of each year's productivity growth was used to improve social
security programs, expand private health and pension benefits, and
raise the relative incomes of the most disadvantaged; yet, there remained enough to allow a significant general increase in real disposable or spendable incomes. Thus, it was possible to mediate among
competing groups by promising more to some without actually reducing incomes of others. Such methods of avoiding direct social
conflict will be far more limited in an economy with little or no

---

10. Surprisingly, this accelerated growth of the employment-to-population ratio reflects
increases in the number of self-employed workers, not an expansion of wage and salary jobs.

11. This result is also in contrast to the common view that inflation has pushed tax-
payers into higher tax brackets. The 1970s, however, was a period of several major tax cuts.

growth. Against this backdrop, it will be more difficult to garner support for regulatory programs that individuals may perceive as further reducing their real incomes. This will be true even if their benefits exceed the costs they are forced to bear because the beneficial effects of regulation may be less obvious than price or output effects.

Specifically, policy measures designed to improve productivity may require that a larger portion of the nation's current production be directed into capital formation, and research and development. It is evident that the productivity slowdown involves far more than just a reduced rate of capital formation. Much of the slowdown must lie with factors such as a reduced rate of technological progress, smaller gains from economies of scale, and special problems in individual industries. But capital formation is one of the few determinants of productivity growth that government policy can influence. The need for increased capital formation is reinforced by the failure of industrial capacity to expand during the 1970s, in contrast with the sharp growth of the labor force. Since that spending cannot expect to be reflected in any increased productivity benefits for several years, it will be sought against a background of small or nonexistent gains in consumer incomes, and a rising level of demands for more resources in areas such as defense spending, energy production, and payments for a growing retirement population.

Changing Competitive Advantage

Inflation and the policies used to restrain it have both had differential impacts on wages and prices in various industries. Some groups are more successful than others in adjusting their incomes for inflation, and there is a wide variation among markets in the sensitivity of prices and wage rates to changes in demand and supply. One consequence has been a major shift in the distribution of wages across industries.[12] This has significant implications for the competitive position of some U.S. industries.

The role of relative wage changes is well illustrated for two industries whose competitive problems have attracted considerable public attention: automobiles and steel. Certainly a complete evaluation of the decline in their competitive positions would have to take account of many factors. Management has made mistakes in anticipating future market trends. The sharp decline in ocean freight rates reduced the competitive advantage of the domestic steel industry with respect to location near markets and raw materials. The shift away from large

---

12. B. Bosworth, Inflation and Relative Wage Rates (paper presented at Ontario Economic Council's Conference on Stagflation, Toronto, Ontario, Nov. 1980).

cars removed what had heretofore been a major trade barrier for foreign auto producers—without a home market base, they could not realize the economies of scale required to compete effectively in selling larger cars. As a final contribution to their problems, both industries have been slow to adopt new technology.

Although it has not attracted much attention, I believe that a sharp change in the relative wages paid in the auto and steel industries is an important element in the trade problems they have experienced. Relative wages (inclusive of fringe benefits and employment taxes) for the steel and automotive industries are shown in Figure 1. Compared with wages in all industries, wages in steel and autos are rising and it is difficult to explain this by normal models of competitive markets: both industries have experienced substantial declines in employment over the past decade. The very sharp rise in steel industry wages results in part from the effort to formulate a rule for adjusting wages for periods stretching beyond the formal three-year contract in return for a no-strike pledge. Currently, total hourly employment costs in automobiles and steel are in excess of $18 per hour, compared with about $11 per hour for all of manufacturing. This has had a doubly sharp effect on automobile prices because of the importance of steel as an input in production.

This shift in relative wage rates reflects the structure of labor markets in the steel and auto industries. Wage rates display little or no sensitivity to changes in demand conditions. Instead, these industries rely heavily upon formal and informal rules for adjusting wages (covering periods longer than that of a formal contract) as a means of avoiding continual conflicts between employers and employees. The adoption of such rules is not limited to these two industries, being relatively common in large impersonal establishments; but steel and autos are more exposed than most to foreign competition.

Such a practice is most evident in the 1946 adoption within the automobile industry of a formal rule for determining wage increases that has changed very little in 30 years: the wage increase is equal to an annual productivity increment plus cost of living. That is, it is a form of indexing, but on a much broader basis than inflation alone. Throughout the 1950s and 1960s, this was quite a reasonable rule and was adopted implicitly and explicitly in many other industries.[13] As long as the productivity increment was closely related to the economy-wide average of 3 percent maintained between 1948 and 1966, it simply increased auto workers' wages in parallel with the rest of the economy. But two things happened to upset the balance of this

---

13. *Id.* at 13-16.

FIGURE 1
Relative wage rate trends.

(Industry compensation divided by that of total manufacturing) (Source: Computed from data of the American Iron and Steel Institute, General Motors, and the National Income Accounts. Compensation includes employment taxes and fringe benefits, and the hours are hours worked rather than paid.)

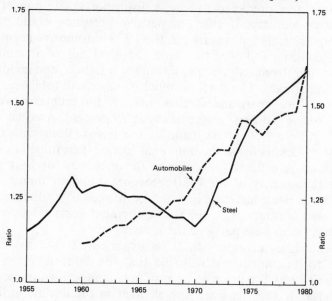

relationship during the 1970s. First, the growth of productivity slowed sharply from 3 percent to about 2 percent annually in the 1967–73 period, 1 percent between 1973 and 1979, and it has actually been negative in the past two years.[14] Second, the consumer price index, to which these wages were tied, began to include a substantial element of external inflation—that is, a decline in the terms of trade as a result of higher food, energy, and land prices, as well as devaluation of the dollar. On average, domestic workers cannot be compensated for such cost increases, which originate from outside the domestic economy unless other factor shares decline. Thus, while the average real wage of the typical factory worker actually declined between 1969 and 1979, the real wage of workers in the auto and steel industries continued to rise at past trends.

The persistence of these wage rules in the face of changing economic circumstances is particularly evident in the 1979 automotive

---

14. ECONOMIC REPORT OF THE PRESIDENT 69 (1981).

contract. Prior to the negotiation, the auto workers' relative wage rate had increased from 1.25 times that of all manufacturing workers in the early 1960s to 1.5 times the average in the late 1970s; thus, there should have been no call for a catch-up for past inflation. Unemployment was high and rising and the industry was facing severe competitive pressures from foreign producers. The upcoming recession was widely predicted to have a disproportionate impact on the automotive industry. If ever competitive pressures would point toward wage restraint, it was true in the 1979 automotive negotiations. Yet the contract followed the same historical rule of an annual productivity improvement, compensation for inflation, and maintenance of existing fringes. The total nominal increase will total near 40 percent over three years and further increase the premium over other manufacturing workers' wages to about 75 percent. An even stronger case for restraint could be made in the negotiations with Chrysler where the workers faced the imminent loss of their jobs. The only result was an agreement to postpone the increases for four months. Despite the severity of the 1980 recession, it had no impact on automotive wage rates, increases in which continued to be dictated by the prior year's contract. Yet, the unemployment costs extended far beyond those who were party to the agreement.

In general, an economy that has experienced excessive inflation relative to its competitors will find that the depreciation of its currency will keep the price of its products competitive in world markets. Certainly this has been one element in the decline in the value of the dollar during the past decade. A decline in the exchange rate to offset increases in the economy-wide average wage rate, however, is not sufficient to afford protection to the automobile and steel industries.

The high relative wage rates in autos and steel would cause no particular competitive problem if they were matched by a similar wage structure in other countries. This is not true, however. The range of variation in relative wages is much narrower in other countries. In steel, only the Japanese wage differential approaches that of the United States and in automobiles no other country is close. There is also no common trend of changing relative wage rates in other countries comparable to that of the United States. In fact, one striking aspect of the international comparisons is that the United States has a far wider distribution of relative wage rates than other countries. Whereas that for the United States ranges from 60 to 160 percent of the manufacturing average, the range for other countries is a more narrow 80 to 125 percent.[15]

---

15. B. Bosworth, *supra* note 12, at 18.

Given equal access to capital and technology, it is difficult to believe that the United States can compete with other countries where wage rates are far below those here. It is equally important to remember, however, that this is a special problem for certain industries and not a general condition of the overall economy. Losses in autos and steel have been offset by the gains of other industries, such as textiles, which now find that their low relative wages improve their competitive position. Of course, while workers in these industries have jobs, many can't afford to buy an American automobile.

What does the behavior of relative wages in the automobile and steel industries imply about regulation? Like the problems of inflation and slow productivity growth, it seems to indicate a difficult period in which to launch new initiatives or perhaps even maintain the stringency of some existing rules. The difficulties faced by the auto and steel industries will place increasing pressure on government to provide some form of assistance to them. Naturally, industry will identify external factors such as regulation and foreign competition as the cause of its problems, rather than internal factors such as wage settlements or the quality of its management. Hence, the likelihood of pushes for regulatory relaxation and protection against imports.

This pattern will not apply across all industries, of course. For example, one industry heavily affected by environmental regulation—electric utilities—cannot claim the threat of foreign competition.[16] Nevertheless, they will no doubt try to pin on regulations some of the blame for poor profitability that may result from overestimation of capacity needs or other internal causes. The challenge across all industries, of course, is a clear one. It is to separate as best we can the effects of regulation from those of the many other factors influencing industry and firm performance. Only when this is done will it be possible to weigh the legitimacy of plans for regulatory relief.

SUMMARY

In the years after the 1974–75 inflation shocks, Japan and Western Europe adopted more restrained economic policies that sharply slowed their rate of growth. Only the United States among the major developed countries attempted to return to the pre-1973 growth path. Western Europe adjusted to lower growth by a variety of different measures. It reversed the previous inflow of foreign guest workers and cut the length of the work week. In addition, most of these

---

16. They can point and have pointed, however, to environmental restrictions on coal use as rendering them more dependent on foreign sources of the energy used to generate their output.

countries experienced a slowdown in productivity growth equal to or greater than that of the United States;[17] but, because their prior rate was so much higher, their lower growth rate placed smaller pressures on real incomes. By all of these measures, other industrial countries were able to minimize the domestic unemployment and political pressures associated with a reduced rate of economic expansion.

The growing difficulties with inflation in recent years now seem to have driven the United States into a policy of slower growth in step with that of other countries. The United States is likely to face far greater difficulties, however, in adjusting to the consequences of that policy. It cannot export its unemployment, which is already high, to other countries; and the continuation of slower productivity growth will have more dramatic implications for real income growth. Since the United States has far more heterogeneous population than many other industrialized nations, the tensions among competing interest groups for an increased share of a slowly growing pie are likely to be more severe.

The clear implication for environmental regulation is that there will be an intensified competition for the use of economic resources. This makes it more important than ever that environmental goals be pursued in cost-effective ways. The use of economic incentives in regulation is one way to accomplish this goal. While these tools are the subject of the final paper in this volume, one point is worth emphasizing here. The more we can reduce the costs associated with a given regulation, the greater are its chances of passing a rigorous cost-benefit test. Given the outlook for the 1980s, this test will play a larger role in the fate of all regulations, new and old.

17. Lawrence, *Keeping Up with the Mitsubishis*, in EXECUTIVE 24-25 (Spring 1980).

The Macroeconomic Impacts of Federal Environmental Regulation

PAUL R. PORTNEY*

As the introduction to this volume points out, environmental and other "social" regulation is suspected of being partly responsible for current economic problems in the United States.[1] This article discusses the expenditures necessitated by federal environmental regulations and the effects of these expenditures on prices, employment, real output, foreign trade, and other measures of economic performance. Because of the breadth of this subject, however, and the great number of studies addressing one or another aspect of it, attention here is focused on the use of large-scale, quarterly econometric models of the United States to examine these effects.[2] While these macroeconomic analyses perforce devote less attention to specific effects—say, those of regulation on trade—than do studies concentrating on single issues, they are comprehensive and integrated, and are of value for that reason.

The first part of this article discusses estimates of expenditures by households, industry, and governmental units that are required in order to comply with federal environmental regulation. The difference between these expenditures and the broader notion of the social

---

*Paul R. Portney is a senior fellow in the Quality of the Environment Division, Resources for the Future.

1. "Social" regulation is usually taken to mean that practiced by the Environmental Protection Agency, the Occupational Safety and Health Administration, the Consumer Product Safety Commission, the Food and Drug Administration, and the National Highway Transportation and Safety Administration. It is sometimes contrasted with what is now called "economic" regulation—that governing price and entry, as exemplified by the Interstate Commerce Commission, the Civil Aeronautics Board, and the Federal Communications Commission.

This distinction between social and economic regulation is an artificial and misleading one, however. Just as economic regulation is intended to correct one kind of market failure —natural monopoly—social regulation is intended to address another—that arising from externalities or imperfect information. Therefore, there is nothing inherently "uneconomic" about social regulation.

2. Other authors have considered a wide range of different methods of determining the economic impact of environmental regulations. *See, e.g.,* G. Christainsen, F. Gollop, & R. Haveman, Environmental and Health-Safety Regulations, Productivity Growth, and Economic Performance: an Assessment (1980) (report prepared for the Office of Technology Assessment of the Joint Economic Committee of the United States Congress). For a comprehensive analysis of the effects of air pollution controls, *see* A. Rose, Assessing the Economic Impact of Air Pollution Abatement (March 1981) (working paper no. 53, Department of Economics, University of California at Riverside).

costs of regulation is also discussed. Because of the importance of expenditure estimates for macroeconomic simulation studies—what goes in, after all, in large part determines what comes out—special attention is given to the difficulties inherent in making such estimates. The second part of the paper, "Models and Results," reviews the methodology employed and results obtained in prior studies of the macroeconomic effects of regulation. The last section discusses the limitations of these macroeconomic studies, the care with which the results should be interpreted, and the ways in which future studies can be improved.

The final section of the paper, as well as the two that precede it, should impart a clear message to readers: while they are valuable if interpreted carefully, the macroeconomic simulation studies discussed are limited in what they can tell us. This is due to the limitations of econometric models and the unavoidably flawed expenditure estimates that drive them. Both these problems receive considerable attention in this article, but it is useful to highlight them here.

SPENDING FOR POLLUTION CONTROL

The econometric models discussed in the second section are defined in terms of the aggregates recorded in the national income and product accounts.[3] That is, the models are driven in large part by the expenditure decisions of households, private businesses, and federal, state, and local governments. Therefore, before these models can be used to evaluate the effects of environmental regulation, the "input" to the models must first be specified. In other words, it must be determined which commercial and industrial establishments, households, and governmental units will be affected by the regulations in question; how much, if anything, they will have to spend to comply with the regulations, and over what period of time; and how they will go about meeting these expenditures.[4]

Expenditures and Costs

To this point I have been careful to refer to the data which drive the simulation studies as pollution control *expenditures* rather than pollution control *costs*. To the layman, this distinction may seem unnecessary. Nevertheless, pollution control expenditures may be

---

3. For a discussion of these accounts, *see* Peskin's paper in this volume.
4. For example, will government finance pollution control expenditures by increasing taxes or by reducing other expenditures? Will business pay for pollution control by additional borrowing, out of retained earnings, or through the issuance of stock?

greater than or less than pollution control costs as economists define them.[5] The size of both is important.

To illustrate the difference between these two concepts, suppose a firm purchases pollution control equipment mandated by law and hires people to operate and maintain it. Part of the expenditures the firm makes includes the sales taxes on the equipment it purchases as well as the payroll taxes it pays for its employees. However, while properly counted as pollution control expenditures, these tax payments are not social or opportunity costs of pollution control because they do not preclude other uses. Rather, these tax payments are transfers from the firm to the government, which uses them for other purposes. In some cases, then, observed pollution control expenditures can exceed the social cost of pollution control.

However, the opportunity cost of pollution control can also be greater than expenditures on pollution control. For example, when firms devote land they already own to pollution control, they do not make an expenditure but they certainly do incur a cost—the forgone use of the land.[6] The social cost of pollution control is equal to observed direct expenditures plus the forgone opportunities from the use of the land.

The social or economic cost of pollution control can diverge from direct expenditures in other important ways. For instance, when a firm installs pollution control equipment, it must generally increase its prices to offset at least part of the increased capital and operating cost.[7] When this increase is reflected in higher final product prices, some consumers will postpone or forgo purchases they would have made at the earlier, lower prices. When this happens, another "hidden" social cost arises that is nowhere reflected in pollution control expenditures—this is the loss in what economists call "consumers' surplus," a loss properly counted in the social costs of pollution control. This loss arises because consumers are generally willing to pay somewhat more for the goods they buy than the prices they are ac-

---

5. To economists, costs are opportunities forgone. Thus, the true economic cost of pollution control is measured by what might have been done with the resources had they been put to their highest and best use.

6. For discussion and analysis of the use of tax-exempt bonds for pollution control, *see* G. Peterson & H. Galper, *Tax Exempt Financing of Private Industry's Pollution Control Investment*, 23 PUB. POL'Y (1975). This provision does not drive a wedge between expenditures and costs, but it does create a disparity between the private and social costs of pollution control.

7. If the firm faces foreign or domestic competition that does not also incur such costs, it may have to pay for pollution control out of reduced factor payments or profits. Generally, however, most producers will face cost increases, hence prices will rise to cover at least part of these higher costs.

tually charged—this excess is consumers' surplus. When high prices choke off demand, those no longer buying the product lose any consumers' surplus they would have enjoyed on the units they would have bought. This forgone opportunity for gain, then, is an economic or social cost of pollution control. The appendix to this article attempts to estimate for a particular case how large this forgone consumers' surplus may be in relation to recorded expenditures on pollution control in one industry.

While it is important to distinguish between expenditures and costs, each concept has its uses. As suggested above, expenditure data are used in both macro- and microeconomic analyses of the effects of regulation on inflation, unemployment, economic growth, and other aggregates. Data on expenditures can also be used to modify the conventional national income and product accounts to reflect the role of environmental protection on gross national product (GNP).[8] Also, estimates of the size and timing of future pollution control expenditures can help indicate where and when difficulties might arise in financing these expenditures. They might indicate whether, for example, public and private borrowing for pollution control will "crowd out" other potential borrowing.

Estimates of the social or resource costs of pollution control, on the other hand, are used in evaluating the welfare effects of environmental regulation. It is the resource or opportunity cost of pollution control that is compared with individuals' willingness to pay for resulting environmental quality in properly done cost-benefit analyses. As indicated in the introduction to this volume, it is this comparison of benefits and costs that indicates the desirability of a regulation or set of regulations from the standpoint of economic efficiency. Macroeconomic studies like those to be discussed later help to understand the way some of the costs of regulation are manifested in the economy. By determining whether unemployment, higher prices, or some combination of these and other effects will result from regulation, we can assess its distributional as well as its allocative effects.

Before turning to the available evidence on pollution control expenditures, one other distinction is worth drawing—that between incremental and total expenditures. Here, incremental expenditures are those that are made in response to federal environmental regulations.[9] Coupled with voluntary spending for pollution control and spending

---

8. *See* note 3, *supra*.
9. Of course, expenditures can be incremental to whatever baseline one desires. Since we are interested here in the effects of federal environmental regulation, that is the increment we consider.

necessitated by state and local rules and regulations, these incremental expenditures combine to form total pollution abatement expenditures. When econometric models are used to determine the impact of federal environmental regulations, incremental expenditures are the appropriate data to consider. If total expenditures were to be used, they might overstate considerably the effect of federal regulation.

Survey Estimates of Expenditures

Considering their importance, there are surprisingly few comprehensive estimates available of either past or future expenditures for pollution control. Sometimes the information that is available is conflicting or disparate. For example, both the Bureau of Economic Analysis (BEA) and the Bureau of the Census within the Department of Commerce conduct annual surveys to determine expenditures on pollution control. Similarly, McGraw-Hill Incorporated also surveys businesses annually to determine pollution abatement expenditures. Table 1 compares estimates from these three sources of actual capital investment in pollution abatement or control for 1978, and estimates from McGraw-Hill and BEA of planned capital expenditures for 1980.

As columns 1, 2, and 3 of the table indicate, there are considerable differences between estimates, even with respect to actual or historical capital expenditures. For example, McGraw-Hill's estimate of pollution control investment in the machinery industry in 1978 is three times that of the Census Bureau, and more than twice that of BEA. On the other hand, the Census estimate for investment in pollution control by the chemical industry is about 50 percent greater than the estimates of either McGraw-Hill or BEA. BEA's estimate for petroleum refining is more than three times that of the Census Bureau, and is 50 percent higher than McGraw-Hill's reported total. Other differences in both individual industry and total estimates are clear.

Given the discrepancies among estimates of historical expenditures for pollution abatement capital, one might expect even more divergent estimates of planned future expenditures. Columns 4 and 5 of Table 1 confirm this suspicion. According to McGraw-Hill, total planned capital expenditures for pollution abatement for all business in 1980 were $10.5 billion. This was 37 percent more than BEA projected based on its survey of manufacturing and nonmanufacturing firms. For the electric utility industry alone, the McGraw-Hill and BEA estimates of 1980 investment in pollution control differed by nearly a billion dollars. Differences like these can influence results of macroeconomic simulation studies, especially when the industry and

TABLE 1

ESTIMATED CAPITAL EXPENDITURES FOR POLLUTION CONTROL
(millions of dollars)

Industry	1978 ACTUAL			1980 PLANNED	
	(1) McG-Hill[a]	(2) BEA[b]	(3) Census[c]	(4) McG-Hill[d]	(5) BEA[b]
Iron and steel	$425	$441	⎰$793	$1069	$638
Nonferrous metals	293	247	⎱	285	285
Other primary metals	–	64		–	87
Electric machinery	134	130	75	238	126
Machinery	243	111	82	196	97
Autos, trucks, parts	193	198	⎰140	162	311
Aerospace	45	23	⎱	30	34
Fabricated metals	137	–		189	–
Instruments	58	–		146	–
Stone	207	164	127	126	176
Other durables	190	181	186	116	199
Total durables	1935	1561	1402	2559	1956
Chemicals	547	565	842	762	476
Paper/pulp	274	239	342	473	300
Rubber	100	58	28	201	58
Petroleum	834	1294	420	1625	1536
Food/Beverage	309	172	185	181	150
Textiles	81	29	60	110	36
Other nondurables	67	32	37	97	27
Total nondurables	2212	2389	1914	3450	2583
Total manufacturing	4147	3950	3316	6009	4540
Mining	511	206		109	171
Railroads	54	36		53	32
Airlines	20	15		97	13
Electric utilities	2791	2472		3615	2658
Gas utilities	60	35		61	44
Commercial	⎱423	⎱210		512	⎱243
Commercial & other trans.	⎰	⎰		93	⎰
	3859	2974		4539	3161
ALL BUSINESS	8006	6924		10,548	7699

Note: Dashes indicate no separate entry.

[a]12th Annual McGraw-Hill Survey of Pollution Control Expenditures, May 14, 1979.

[b]Gary Rutledge and Betsy O'Connor, "Capital Expenditures by Business for Pollution Abatement, 1978, 1979, and Planned 1980," *Survey of Current Business*, June 1980.

[c]*Pollution Abatement Costs and Expenditures, 1978*, U.S. Bureau of the Census, MA-200(78)-2, U.S. G.P.O., Washington, D.C., 1980.

[d]13th Annual McGraw-Hill Survey.

product in question is, like electricity, an important factor in the production of other goods.

There are two major reasons why these three sets of estimates diverge so. First, the Census Bureau surveys establishments or plants, while the BEA survey goes to firms. Hence, if a multidivision firm has operations in several different industries, *all* of its pollution control expenditures across all operations are attributed by BEA to its primary product. Thus, expenditures for pollution control in U.S. Steel's paintmaking operations are recorded under "steel works" in the BEA survey. This accounts for some of the differences between BEA and Census. Second, the sample sizes used by BEA, Census, and McGraw-Hill differ. The Census Bureau surveys 20,000 plants to estimate pollution control investment in the manufacturing sector. The Bureau of Economic Analysis surveys about 15,000 firms to prepare its estimate. McGraw-Hill, like BEA, bases its estimates on a sample of firms, yet they sample only 346—less than 3 percent of BEA's sample size. Hence, all three sources are trying to estimate national totals based on different sample sizes, composition, and definitions.

Several factors point toward possible upward bias of all three sets of estimates. Although the response rates for the McGraw-Hill and Census surveys are unknown, it is about 60 percent for BEA, of which at least some responses no doubt prove unusable. It is not unreasonable to expect that the firms that do respond to the survey are those that are spending considerable amounts on pollution abatement. If their experience is generalized to all firms in an industry, the resulting estimates will be high. This will be particularly true in industries with both large firms and small firms. Since many regulations exempt firms below a certain size, the effect of environmental rules on all small firms taken together could be negligible. Yet, if a number of small firms are treated as one big firm, estimates of their expenditures may be large.

Second, some respondents can be expected to have difficulty determining which portion of capital and operating expenditures is due to pollution abatement and which portion is made to improve normal operations and increase profitability. This joint cost problem is especially difficult when new facilities are constructed or existing ones are modified. The temptation in such cases is to err in the direction of large pollution control expenditures, creating a possible further upward bias to the estimates. Finally, although there is little evidence to support such a supposition, some firms may deliberately report erroneously high numbers in an attempt to cast regulation in a bad light.[10]

Engineering Estimates of Expenditures

In its annual report to the President, the Council on Environmental Quality (CEQ) also makes an estimate of total spending in the previous year on pollution abatement and control. Unlike that of the Bureau of Economic Analysis, CEQ's estimate is not based on survey data, although it has made some use of BEA analyses in preparing its estimates. Rather, the CEQ estimates are known as engineering estimates. They are based on assumptions about the type of equipment that will be required to comply with regulations, the cost of that equipment, and the number of sources that will have to install it. For example, the CEQ estimates assume that scrubbers will be required to meet new source performance standards governing sulfur dioxide emissions from coal-fired electric utilities. Similarly, it is assumed that certain existing utilities and other industrial sources will be forced to burn more expensive low-sulfur fuel oil and coal. With respect to land reclamation, the estimates assume that certain equipment will be required in order to restore strip-mined land to its approximate original contour. The cost of this equipment and its operation, then, more or less determine the resulting cost estimates.

Table 2 compares CEQ and BEA estimates of total spending between 1973 and 1978 for air and water pollution control and solid waste disposal. As the table indicates, in recent years the CEQ and BEA estimates have not differed by more than 10 percent and the cumulative totals over the six-year period 1973–78 are within 3 percent of each other.

Because BEA's estimates do not differentiate between incremental and total expenditures, they are not useful for determining the macroeconomic consequences of federal regulation. However, CEQ estimates not only total pollution control expenditures in each year, but also those expenditures which arose because of federal environmental regulations. Moreover, each year CEQ estimates incremental and total environmental quality expenditures over the next decade. These include, not only expenditures for air and water pollution control and solid waste disposal, but also those for the control of noise, pesticides, and toxic substances; for the protection of drinking water; and for land reclamation following surface and underground mining.

---

10. For an analysis of possible ways to elicit accurate and honest cost information from firms, *see* J. Sonstelie, Economic Incentives and the Revelation of Compliance Costs (1981) (report prepared for the Council on Environmental Quality, Washington, D.C.).

TABLE 2

ESTIMATED TOTAL EXPENDITURES ON POLLUTION CONTROL:
AIR, WATER, AND SOLID WASTE*
(billions of current dollars)

Year	BEA[a]	CEQ[b]
1973	$22.3	$14.8
1974	26.2	21.6
1975	30.6	31.7
1976	34.2	34.2
1977	37.5	39.8
1978	42.3	45.9
Total	$193.1	$188.0

*Includes voluntary pollution abatement expenditures, those necessitated by state and local regulation, and those necessitated by federal environmental regulation.

[a]Gary Rutledge and Susan Trevathan, "Pollution Abatement and Control Expenditures, 1972–78," *Survey of Current Business,* February 1980, pp. 27–33.

[b]*Environmental Quality,* 1974, p. 221; *EQ,* 1975, p. 564; *EQ,* 1976, p. 167; *EQ,* 1977, p. 334; *EQ,* 1978, p. 447; *EQ,* 1979, p. 667.

In addition to these efforts, EPA is directed in the Clean Air Act and the Clean Water Act to make an annual reporting of the expenditures necessary to carry out those acts. This requirement has resulted in the publication of several such reports, the most recent of which appeared in 1979.[11] These reports deal only with air and water pollution control, although by definition they do report incremental rather than total expenditures. One major difficulty with the EPA estimates (which also are based on the engineering approach) is that they are generally out of date by the time they appear. For example, the August 1979 report did not include the effects on future incremental expenditures of the 1977 amendments to either the Clean Air Act or the Clean Water Act. Hence, the EPA estimates would have to be supplemented with additional information if they were to be used to determine the effect on the economy of current federal air or water pollution control efforts.

In fact, the estimates of air and water pollution control expenditures that CEQ reports in its most recent annual report are based in part on EPA's 1979 *Cost of Clean Air and Water,* but are augmented to take account of changes in the law and the promulgation of new

11. *See* U.S. ENVT'L PROTECTION AGENCY, THE COST OF CLEAN AIR AND WATER: A REPORT TO CONGRESS (1979).

rules and regulations between 1977 and 1979. Because CEQ's annual estimate of incremental expenditures is more current with respect to air and water pollution control than EPA's, and includes additional information as well, it is presented in Table 3. Note that expenditures are estimated for 1979, 1988, and cumulatively for the decade in between.

Several observations about the CEQ estimates are in order. First, in absolute terms, estimated expenditures on pollution abatement and environmental quality are quite substantial. The $37 billion that CEQ estimates was spent to comply with all federal environmental regulation in 1979 was about three-fourths of all federal spending on health care in the United States in that year and 62 percent of total U.S. payments for imported oil in 1979. Thus, environmental regulation requires considerably more than slight changes in the operating practices of households, businesses, and governments.

This trend is likely to continue, according to CEQ. By 1988, expenditures for pollution abatement and other environmental quality programs will grow to nearly $70 billion in constant (1979) dollars. This represents an estimated annual real rate of growth of 6.6 percent, at least twice and perhaps three times the rate of growth expected for the economy as a whole during this period. This comparison between overall economic growth on the one hand and expenditures necessitated by federal environmental regulation on the other, helps put these expenditures in a somewhat different light. For while clearly large in absolute terms, environmental control expenditures still account for a fairly small fraction of gross national product—less than 1.6 percent in 1979. If real GNP grows at a rate of 2 percent until 1988, the ratio of federally induced environmental spending to real gross national product will still be less than 2.5 percent.

For the purposes of this discussion, these ratios have additional significance. Because macroeconomic models are driven by expenditures for all purposes, and because the ratio of incremental expenditures for pollution control to GNP is small, we should not expect pollution control expenditures to have a very large direct effect on the macroeconomic aggregates of interest. That is, since expenditures induced by regulation are still small in comparison to the size of the economy, they cannot have a large effect in modeling exercises. This helps explain the results discussed in the next section.

Finally, because the CEQ estimates (and those of EPA upon which they are partially based) are engineering estimates, they, too, must be interpreted cautiously. First, the engineering approach has its own inherent bias toward overestimation. Over time, it is inevitable that

TABLE 3

ESTIMATED INCREMENTAL POLLUTION ABATEMENT EXPENDITURES,[a] 1979–88*

(billions of 1979 dollars)

Program	1979			1988			Cumulative (1979–88)		
	Operation and maintenance	Annual capital costs[b]	Total annual costs	Operation and maintenance	Annual capital costs[b]	Total annual costs	Operation and maintenance	Capital costs[b]	Total costs
Air pollution									
Public	1.2	.3	1.5	2.0	.5	2.5	15.7	3.7	19.5
Private									
Mobile	3.2	4.9	8.1	3.7	11.0	14.7	32.1	83.7	115.8
Industrial	2.0	2.3	4.3	3.0	4.1	7.1	25.8	33.0	58.8
Electric utilities	5.5	2.9	8.4	7.6	5.7	13.3	62.3	42.7	105.0
Subtotal	11.9	10.4	22.3	16.3	21.3	37.6	136.0	163.1	299.1
Water pollution									
Public	1.7	4.3	6.0	3.3	10.0	13.3	25.1	59.2	84.3
Private									
Industrial	3.4	2.6	6.0	5.4	4.5	9.9	42.0	34.0	76.0
Electric utilities	.3	.4	.7	.3	.9	1.2	2.9	6.5	9.4
Subtotal	5.4	7.3	12.7	9.0	15.4	24.4	70.0	99.7	169.7
Solid waste									
Public	<.05	<.05	<.05	.4	.3	.7	2.6	2.0	4.6
Private	<.05	<.05	<.05	.9	.7	1.6	6.4	4.4	10.8
Subtotal	<.05	<.05	<.05	1.3	1.0	2.3	9.0	6.4	15.4
Toxic substances	.1	.2	.3	.5	.6	1.1	3.6	4.6	8.2
Drinking water	<.05	<.05	<.05	.1	.3	.4	1.3	1.4	2.7
Noise	<.05	.1	.1	.6	1.0	1.6	2.6	4.3	6.9
Pesticides	.1	<.05	.1	.1	<.05	.1	1.2	<.05	1.2
Land reclamation	.3	1.1	1.4	.3	1.2	1.5	3.8	11.5	15.3
Total	17.8	19.1	36.9	28.2	40.8	69.0	227.5	291.0	518.5

*Source: COUNCIL ON ENVT'L QUALITY, ELEVENTH ANNUAL REPORT 394 (1980).

[a] Incremental costs are those made in response to federal environmental legislation beyond those that would have been made in the absence of the legislation.

[b] Interest and depreciation.

new, less expensive means will be developed to meet environmental standards (for example, dry scrubbers and fluidized bed combustion for sulfur dioxide removal, as opposed to the wet scrubbers assumed in the estimates). Hence, actual pollution control expenditures should fall over time relative to engineering estimates of expenditures, as a result of technological innovation.

Second, actual expenditures (and costs) may fall short of engineering estimates as a result of what might be called regulatory innovation. By this I mean the redesign or reform of regulation to allow for greater flexibility in compliance.[12] EPA's "bubble" and "offset" policies are examples of this increased flexibility. Respectively, they allow individual firms to reduce pollution in the least expensive ways, and permit reductions in emissions in geographic areas to take place in locations where pollution control can be most easily accommodated. In this way, regulatory innovation can act to spur technological innovation. As more and better use is made of economic incentives and other innovative approaches to regulation, actual expenditures and costs can be expected to fall short of ex ante, engineering estimates.

A third reason why engineering estimates can be regarded as no more than broadly suggestive has to do with the open-endedness of many rules and the discretion they give to EPA. For example, Section 112 of the Clean Air Act authorizes EPA to identify and establish emissions limitations for hazardous air pollutants. Similarly, the Toxic Substances Control Act empowers EPA to establish testing requirements for many new or existing chemicals and to ban certain substances found to pose hazards to human health. Neither in these nor in other cases can we be sure of the eventual number of substances that will be controlled, the stringency of these controls, the ease with which they can be met, and their subsequent economic effects. Yet such information is necessary to determine, for simulation or other purposes, the expenditures likely to arise as a result of regulation. For these three reasons, then, the CEQ/EPA expenditure estimates should be viewed with the same caution as those based on surveys of firms or industrial plants.

Summary

What are we to conclude from all this? What is the relationship between expenditures on pollution control and the economic or social costs arising from regulation? Do existing estimates understate pollution control costs and expenditures? Can the expenditure estimates be used in macroeconomic simulations to identify aggregate impacts?

---

12. *See* the paper by Harrington and Krupnick in this volume.

The following inferences seem warranted. First, the social cost of environmental regulation is probably greater, and perhaps significantly so, than actual direct expenditures for pollution control. This follows from the important costs of pollution control that are omitted from expenditure estimates (see the appendix for a rough calculation of some of these costs). These omissions probably offset the occasional divergence between private and social costs that can cause expenditures to exceed resource costs.

Second, although costs probably exceed actual direct expenditures, both are likely to fall short of most estimates of expenditures, quite possibly by a considerable margin. Existing survey estimates are based on responses from those firms or plants likely to be the most severely affected by regulations. These respondents also have incentives to err on the high side when reporting their expenditures for pollution control. Engineering cost estimates can also be expected to frequently overstate pollution control expenditures because it is difficult to foresee the technological changes that will reduce compliance costs and expenditures over time. Neither can the possible regulatory innovations that will arise be foreseen.

Still, existing expenditure estimates are not without value. They do provide the information necessary to run the macroeconomic models. They do enable us, in this way, to determine roughly how the costs of regulation may manifest themselves in the economy. This does enable us to draw some inferences about the distributional effects of these regulations. Nevertheless, for the reasons outlined above, expenditure estimates are inevitably flawed and must be recognized as such. They can be viewed as no more than suggestive, and at times they may fall short of even this modest goal.

MODELS AND RESULTS

In addition to helping identify the macroeconomic effects of regulation, the large quarterly models of the U.S. economy have been used to analyze the effects of changes in government tax and expenditure policies, perturbations in the price and availability of energy and other natural resources, changes in consumer and producer behavior, and natural occurrences such as droughts or prolonged periods of hot or cold weather. Econometric models offer two advantages in these and other kinds of studies. The first is their comprehensiveness. That is, they identify effects on many important aggregate measures, such as the inflation rate, the unemployment rate, the trade balance, and new investment, as well as price and output effects for at least some individual economic sectors (the pulp and paper industry, electric utilities, food processing, and so on).

The second attractive feature of the econometric models is that the predictions they generate are integrated and simultaneously determined. The equations of the models are linked so that price increases in one sector are translated into cost and price increases in other sectors. These secondary effects may influence employment in affected industries, which in turn may influence aggregate demand. Similarly, the many other feedbacks inherent in econometric models ensure at least a crude approximation to the simultaneous and interdependent decision-making characterizing a market economy. These feedbacks are missing when piecemeal or partial equilibrium approaches are used to examine the response of a particular industry or sector to a policy or other change. While piecemeal approaches often allow the inclusion of more detail (when one worries about sugar beet processing, for example, one can specify production at the individual process level), they often ignore induced changes in other industries or input markets that might eventually produce results very different from those that emerge from an industry-specific or microanalytic approach.

Design of the Macro Studies

The general approach taken in the macroeconomic simulation studies is easy enough to describe. Beginning with estimates of the expenditures necessitated by regulation, it is first determined how these expenditures will manifest themselves in the economy (or how their absence would be felt). By adjusting the appropriate equations in the model, one can characterize an economy without regulation and the spending it entails. For example, any jobs related to the manufacturing of mandated pollution control equipment must be deleted in the "without controls" case. Similarly, investment in pollution control equipment must be removed, as must state and local spending for pollution abatement. State and local taxes must be reduced by the amount of expenditures in the "without" case, as well. Finally, a basic set of assumptions must be made about the future values of the variables determined outside the model, the so-called exogenous variables. For example, how much will the three levels of government spend for goods and services in the years to come? At what rates will income be taxed? How fast will the money supply expand? What will be the rate of population growth?

Once appropriate adjustments have been made to the model and the exogenous variables have been specified, the model can be solved to produce a picture of the economy operating over some period of time first in the presence, and then in the absence of environmental regulation. The only difference between the two simulations is that one includes spending and other changes induced by regulation, while the other does not. The difference between the time paths of the important variables is then taken to be the measure of the effect of regulation. This is the basic approach that has been used in all the simulation studies to date.

The Chase and DRI Studies

The first such study was conducted in 1972 by Chase Econometric Associates for CEQ, EPA, and the Department of Commerce. There were a number of steps to the Chase methodology, which began with CEQ and EPA estimates of the incremental expenditures in 15 major industries for annualized capital and operations and maintenance expenses. No attempt was made in the study to include estimates of municipal spending on waste treatment.

Chase calculated the initial effects of these expenditures on production costs in the industries considered. These cost increases were then translated into price increases using industry markup factors. Then it was determined how these initial increases would affect costs and prices in other industries through their effects on the prices of inputs to these industries. (For example, the cost of producing automobiles went up not only because of air and water pollution control expenditures by automakers, but also because steelmakers were forced to invest in pollution control.) Next, these direct and indirect increases in the prices of intermediate products were translated into changes in the prices of final products. After adjusting the investment equations of the model as well as the user cost of capital (to reflect the added investment in "unproductive" plants and equipment), the Chase macro model was solved to determine the general equilibrium effects of industrial expenditures on pollution control.

Some of the important results of this study are presented in Table 4. Chase predicted that industrial pollution control expenditures would have a somewhat restrictive effect on the economy over the nine-year period 1972–80. For example, the unemployment rate was predicted to be higher in the presence of environmental controls than without them, averaging about 0.13 of one percentage point per year higher over the eight-year period. During the same period, Chase predicted the inflation rate to be higher in the "with-controls" case for the first four years (by about 0.35 of one percentage point) but then lower than in the baseline (or no-controls case) for the five years 1976

TABLE 4
EFFECTS OF POLLUTION CONTROL ON MACROECONOMIC VARIABLES

	1972	1973	1974	1975	1976	1977	1978	1979	1980
Unemployment rate, percent									
Baseline projection	5.41	4.93	4.70	4.73	4.38	4.37	4.44	4.44	4.47
With pollution control costs	5.39	4.99	4.81	4.90	4.52	4.55	4.61	4.59	4.62
Difference	.02	.06	.11	.17	.14	.18	.17	.15	.15
Percentage growth rate of consumer price index									
Baseline projection	2.97	4.13	4.39	4.48	3.98	4.17	3.96	3.56	3.21
With pollution control costs	3.17	4.47	4.88	4.83	3.87	3.80	3.61	3.29	2.99
Difference	.20	.34	.49	.35	-.11	-.37	-.35	-.27	-.22
Gross national product, constant dollars									
Baseline projection	786.4	836.6	875.7	907.8	954.3	997.3	1038.8	1083.6	1131.5
With pollution control costs	788.4	835.7	872.4	899.4	941.2	984.8	1029.0	1075.0	1123.2
Difference	2.0	-0.9	-3.3	-8.4	-13.1	-12.5	-9.8	-8.6	-8.3
Net foreign balance									
Baseline projection	3.5	3.5	1.6	1.0	0.2	-1.1	-1.1	0.7	3.3
With pollution control costs	2.9	2.7	0.1	-.9	-.8	-1.3	-1.2	.6	3.1
Difference	-.6	-.8	-1.5	-1.9	-1.0	-0.2	-0.1	-0.1	-0.2
Fixed business investment, constant dollars									
Baseline projection	83.6	93.0	101.4	105.7	112.4	118.3	123.3	129.2	135.1
With pollution control costs	85.4	95.0	104.5	108.5	112.3	116.5	121.5	127.7	133.9
Difference	1.8	2.0	3.1	2.8	-0.1	-1.8	-1.8	-1.5	-1.2

Source: Chase Econometric Associates, Inc., "The General Economy," pp. 323–324 in *The Economic Impact of Pollution Control: A Summary of Recent Studies*, prepared for the Council on Environmental Quality, the Department of Commerce, and the Environmental Protection Agency, March 1972.

through 1980. According to Chase, after 1972 real gross national product was expected to be lower throughout the simulation period as a result of pollution control. The difference was expected to be the largest in 1976, when pollution control spending was seen as reducing real GNP by $13.1 billion, or 1.4 percent. As the table indicates, both the balance of trade (net foreign balance) and fixed business investment were predicted to be adversely affected by pollution control spending, although Chase expected the latter to be simulated initially by the pollution control investments firms had to make.

In a number of respects, the 1972 Chase study is quite dated. First, new regulations have imposed added costs on the industries considered. For example, according to the inputs supplied to Chase in 1972, by 1977 the petroleum refining industry would be bearing annual incremental pollution control expenditures of $304 million (in 1978 dollars). However, according to EPA's more recent 1977 *Cost of Clean Air and Water* report, annual incremental expenditures in petroleum refining in 1977 were $682 million, and this excluded any costs associated with the 1977 amendments to the Clean Air and Clean Water acts.

Second, the municipal waste treatment expenditures excluded from the 1972 Chase analysis are significant. According to CEQ, for example, such expenditures amounted to nearly half of all incremental water pollution control spending in 1979 (see Table 3). Hence, by excluding such spending, the Chase study understated the effect of environmental regulation on economic performance. Finally, changes in the structure of the U.S. and world economies since 1972 also help render obsolete Chase's 1972 prediction of the impacts environmental regulation would have on the economy in 1980.

Of course, the best estimates of the current or future effects of environmental regulation will come from those models which are based on the most recent data and representation of the economy. While Chase has continuously updated its model, and used it to reexamine periodically the effects of environmental control expenditures,[13] the most recent econometric study was conducted for CEQ and EPA by Data Resources Incorporated (DRI) in 1978.[14]

In several respects, the 1978 DRI study represents the state of the art for such efforts. First, and perhaps most important, the DRI

---

13. The 1976 Chase study is described and analyzed in some detail in R. Haveman & V. Kerry Smith, *Investment, Inflation, Unemployment, and the Environment*, in CURRENT ISSUES IN U.S. ENVIRONMENTAL POLICY 164 (P. Portney ed. 1978).

14. Data Resources Inc., The Macroeconomic Impact of Federal Pollution Control Programs: 1978 Assessment (Jan. 29, 1979) (report submitted to the Environmental Protection Agency and the Council on Environmental Quality, Washington, D.C.).

study used the most comprehensive and recent estimates of pollution control expenditures. For example, the study was based on CEQ and EPA estimates of incremental air and water pollution control spending between 1970 and 1986. Table 5 presents the EPA/CEQ estimates of incremental investment in pollution control between 1970 and 1986 used in the study, including expenditures for mobile source pollution control and expenditures by states and municipalities for water pollution control. These latter governmental expenditures had never before been included in macro simulation studies.

It is important to note, however, that DRI did not take into account expenditures expected to arise from the 1977 amendments to the Clean Air and Clean Water acts. Hence, the results do not include any of the direct effects on the economy of regulations protecting visibility or air quality in clean areas, or the effects of new controls on industries discharging toxic substances into water bodies. Neither did the inputs to the DRI study include any of the effects of existing regulations governing hazardous wastes, toxic substances, land reclamation, noise control, or drinking water protection. While expenditures for these programs currently are small relative to those made for air and water pollution control, they will grow in time, as Table 3 shows.

The obvious additional advantage of the DRI study is its relatively recent completion. This means that the model used to perform the study reflects at least some of the recent experience with diminished rates of productivity growth, high and unstable energy prices, expansions in labor force participation, and other changes in economic conditions and structural relationships. Data Resources faces the same problems in predicting future economic behavior and relationships as plagued the 1972 Chase effort, of course, but their results do give us the best picture of current effects associated with regulation.

The methodology of the DRI study was similar to that used by Chase.[15] To simulate the absence of air and water pollution control, DRI reduced aggregate investment in durable equipment and in new plant construction and apportioned these reductions across individual industrial sectors. The rental price of capital was also reduced to reflect the fact that no "unproductive" pollution control investment need accompany "productive" investment in the absence of controls.[16] These cost reductions in the no-controls case were then translated into lower final product prices. Personal consumption ex-

15. For a more thorough description of the methodology of Data Resources, Inc., *see id.* (Technical Appendix—submitted to EPA and CEQ March 30, 1979).

16. For a discussion of the national income accounts and what they measure and exclude as productive outputs, *see* Peskin's paper in this volume.

TABLE 5

ESTIMATED INCREMENTAL INVESTMENT FOR POLLUTION CONTROL, 1970–1986

(millions of 1977 dollars)

	1970	1971	1972	1973	1974	1975	1976	1977	1978	1979	1980	1981	1982	1983	1984	1985	1986
All industries	2,458	3,258	4,690	4,848	4,640	5,181	4,946	4,770	4,405	6,643	7,338	6,849	7,402	8,208	8,413	7,216	6,659
Manufacturing industries	1,450	1,931	2,800	2,897	3,092	3,671	3,195	3,013	2,755	3,582	4,095	4,373	4,503	4,907	4,740	4,493	4,337
Primary Metals	269	361	556	587	661	892	753	719	654	804	979	968	950	1,057	572	520	481
Electrical Machinery	14	22	35	36	34	23	25	22	18	37	44	45	51	50	48	45	37
Non-electrical Machinery	10	19	35	37	39	30	34	31	25	45	41	38	32	32	26	19	17
Transportation Equipment	59	75	103	106	94	54	56	53	49	97	137	178	213	252	287	206	219
Stone, Clay & Glass	76	101	157	167	213	157	75	70	62	97	154	217	280	316	378	274	170
Other Durables	47	72	119	125	163	130	91	82	70	99	90	84	82	75	69	62	61
Food Incl. Beverage	117	149	197	200	176	139	168	161	149	400	554	674	749	716	788	796	806
Textiles	16	21	27	27	26	36	43	41	38	94	156	219	241	254	266	270	248
Paper	208	265	356	363	487	572	359	339	317	492	640	638	635	631	629	626	623
Chemicals	251	318	415	420	536	733	847	809	764	931	793	794	798	1,048	1,351	1,852	1,357
Petroleum	373	512	773	800	616	864	702	648	574	415	414	410	348	342	174	194	214
Rubber	2	5	11	12	27	15	18	17	14	34	40	47	54	61	67	53	39
Other Nondurables	9	11	16	17	22	26	24	23	21	37	53	61	69	73	84	75	64
Nonmanufacturing	1,008	1,327	1,889	1,951	1,548	1,510	1,751	1,757	1,649	3,061	3,243	2,476	2,899	3,301	3,674	2,724	2,322
Mining	59	75	98	98	24	63	71	49	47	119	85	54	72	88	102	70	58
Public Utilities	750	999	1,444	1,492	1,398	1,297	1,532	1,569	1,473	2,845	3,061	2,269	2,675	3,060	3,418	2,500	2,109
Commercial	200	253	348	361	126	150	147	140	129	97	97	153	152	154	154	154	155
State and local government	-38	490	310	143	1,378	1,548	2,635	2,310	2,434	2,960	3,190	2,902	2,442	1,888	1,542	1,705	1,778
Mobile source emission control	505	599	581	1,499	1,011	2,123	2,622	2,755	2,728	2,679	3,633	5,430	5,288	5,475	5,667	5,756	5,756

Source: Data Resources Inc., "The Macroeconomic Impact of Federal Pollution Control Programs: 1978 Assessment," p. 9, a report submitted to the Environmental Protection Agency and the Council on Environmental Quality, January 29, 1979.

penditures on automobiles were reduced, since there would be no fuel economy penalty without controls, and new car prices were reduced. Federal grants-in-aid to municipalities (which cover 75 percent of the capital cost of waste treatment plants) were reduced, as were state and local expenditures for waste treatment.

Finally, the share of annual operations and maintenance expenditures devoted to labor—assumed to be 50 percent by DRI[17]—was divided by the average wage in manufacturing. This provided an estimate of the annual increase in jobs resulting from pollution control expenditures. Appropriate adjustments were made to the unemployment rate in the without-controls case (initially raising it above its level in the "with-controls" case).

Table 6 presents some of the major results of the DRI study for the entire seventeen-year simulation period. Consider first the inflation rate, measured by the percentage rate of growth of the consumer price index for urban areas. According to DRI, the effect of air and water pollution controls was to increase the expected inflation rate over the seventeen-year period by an average of 0.25 of one percentage point a year. Between 1970 and 1978, the period over which one can expect the DRI model to be the most accurate (because it was estimated using data from that period), the environmental regulations were seen as adding nearly one-third of one percentage point to the average annual inflation rate. In 1977, for example, the inflation rate in the "with-controls" case was predicted to be 6.5 percent as opposed to 6.2 percent in the absence of controls. Between 1979 and 1986, DRI predicted, air and water pollution controls would add an average of 0.13 of one percentage point to the annual rate of price increases.

According to DRI, air and water pollution control expenditures stimulated employment in the past and will continue to do so through 1986. Between 1970 and 1986, DRI found the average unemployment rate to be lower by 0.25 of a percentage point annually in the with-controls case than in the absence of controls. This difference is about the same in both the estimation period and the 1979–86 forecast period. For 1980 and 1981, DRI estimated that pollution control spending would reduce the unemployment rate by 0.4 of one percentage point.

The effects on unemployment that DRI identified are net effects. That is, DRI predicted that the jobs created by pollution control (in the production, installation, operation, and maintenance of pollution

TABLE 6

ESTIMATED IMPACT OF POLLUTION CONTROL EXPENDITURES ON THE ECONOMY, 1970–86

	1970	1971	1972	1973	1974	1975	1976	1977	1978	1979	1980	1981	1982	1983	1984	1985	1986
Percentage growth rate of CPIU																	
Without	5.8	4.1	3.0	5.8	10.5	8.7	5.4	6.2	7.3	7.0	6.8	6.6	6.0	5.9	5.8	5.8	5.7
With	5.9	4.3	3.3	6.2	11.0	9.1	5.8	6.5	7.5	7.1	6.9	6.8	6.3	6.1	5.9	5.8	5.7
Diff	0.1	0.2	0.3	0.5	0.5	0.4	0.4	0.3	0.2	0.1	0.1	0.3	0.3	0.2	0.1	0.1	0.1
Unemployment rate, percent																	
Without	5.2	6.3	6.0	5.2	5.8	8.6	7.9	7.2	6.2	6.4	6.4	6.2	6.4	6.0	5.4	5.2	5.2
With	5.0	5.9	5.6	4.8	5.6	8.5	7.7	7.0	6.1	6.3	6.0	5.7	6.1	5.7	5.2	5.0	5.0
Diff	-0.2	-0.3	-0.4	-0.3	-0.2	-0.2	-0.2	-0.2	-0.1	-0.2	-0.4	-0.4	-0.3	-0.2	-0.2	-0.2	-0.2
Gross national product, 1977 dollars																	
Without	1515.3	1555.1	1643.8	1737.7	1718.8	1698.2	1793.8	1884.2	1963.6	2021.9	2109.5	2183.5	2252.6	2362.1	2473.7	2563.5	2646.7
With	1522.5	1568.2	1658.3	1748.7	1724.6	1702.6	1799.6	1806.8	1959.9	2023.0	2118.8	2189.7	2250.9	2351.9	2457.0	2543.5	2622.3
Diff	7.2	13.1	14.4	11.0	5.8	4.4	5.8	2.5	-3.7	1.1	9.3	6.2	-1.8	-10.2	-16.7	-20.0	-24.5
Imports, 1977 dollars																	
Without	137.1	141.2	155.3	162.5	157.2	137.5	164.0	180.8	199.9	205.4	215.2	226.2	233.1	245.8	262.4	278.3	292.9
With	138.2	144.1	159.8	167.9	162.2	142.0	169.3	186.6	204.8	210.3	221.6	233.2	239.3	251.2	267.0	282.1	295.6
Diff	1.1	2.9	4.5	5.4	5.0	4.5	5.4	5.8	4.9	5.0	6.4	7.0	6.2	5.4	4.6	3.8	2.7
Exports, 1977 dollars																	
Without	119.8	121.1	129.5	156.0	166.2	161.0	171.6	175.7	189.6	200.6	210.7	222.6	233.0	244.1	255.8	267.9	280.4
With	119.9	121.3	129.9	156.2	166.2	160.9	171.4	175.5	189.0	199.9	210.2	222.0	232.1	242.7	254.0	265.9	278.1
Diff	0.1	0.3	0.3	0.2	0.0	-0.2	-0.2	-0.2	-0.6	-0.7	-0.6	-0.6	-1.0	-1.4	-1.8	-2.0	-2.3

Source: Data Resources Inc., "The Macroeconomic Impact of Federal Pollution Control Programs, 1978 Assessment," submitted to the Environmental Protection Agency and the Council on Environmental Quality, Washington, D.C., January 29, 1979.

control equipment) would more than offset any job losses resulting from regulation-induced slowdowns in economic activity.

Pollution control expenditures were predicted by DRI to have a mixed effect on real GNP between 1970 and 1986. Between 1970 and 1978, according to DRI, real GNP was higher than it would have been without environmental controls. This was due to the stimulating effect of added spending for pollution control, which outweighed the restrictive effects that higher prices and reduced productivity had on the growth of real output. In six of the nine years between 1978 and 1986, however, real GNP was predicted to be lower in the presence of pollution control spending than in its absence. By 1986, in fact, DRI predicted this difference to be $24.5 billion, or nearly 1 percent of predicted real GNP in that year. Over the entire seventeen-year period, according to DRI, pollution control expenditures would produce a cumulative net gain in real GNP of $3.9 billion. Had the simulation period been extended one more year, however, the cumulative net effect on real output would no doubt have been negative, given the large gaps between the two scenarios toward the end of the period.

According to DRI, the balance of trade has been and is likely to be adversely affected by expenditures on pollution control. Imports are predicted to be higher throughout the seventeen-year period on account of controls, the average annual difference being on the order of $4.7 billion. Exports initially increased in the "with-controls" case (from sales of pollution control equipment), although the increase was small and disappeared by 1974. From 1975 on, exports are lower in the with-controls case, the average annual difference amounting to about $1 billion.

While the adverse trade effects of pollution control may be fairly small in absolute terms, they can be a large percentage of the annual trade balance, according to DRI. For example, DRI predicted that the 1980 trade deficit in the "with-controls" case would be $11.4 billion, as opposed to $4.5 billion in the absence of air and water quality legislation. Hence, DRI found that environmental control expenditures would be responsible for about 60 percent of the predicted U.S. trade deficit in 1980.

Since real GNP was generally lower after 1978 in the "with controls" case, even though employment was found to be higher, it follows directly that productivity (or output per person employed) must be less in the "with controls" case. The DRI results, and others bearing on regulation and productivity, are discussed in the paper by Robert Haveman and Gregory Christainsen in this volume.

CONCLUSIONS AND RECOMMENDATIONS

There are a number of observations that can be drawn about the methodologies of the macro studies, the results obtained, and the care with which these results should be interpreted.

First, although the Chase and DRI studies obtain somewhat conflicting results,[18] the studies are in agreement as to the apparent size of the impacts of pollution control. Both find the direct price, output, employment, and other macroeconomic effects of pollution control to be relatively small. This is not to dismiss a contribution to the inflation rate of 0.2 to 0.6 of one percentage point as trivial. It is not. But with inflation rates in excess of 10 percent per year, neither can it be argued that even drastic cutbacks in regulation would make an immediate and substantial contribution to lower prices. The same can be said of the effects of environmental controls on employment or unemployment, the rate of growth of the economy, and so on. To reemphasize, this conclusion follows quite directly from the relatively small size of environmental control expenditures *when compared with GNP.* Given this ratio (currently about 1.5 to 2.0 percent), it would be surprising if environmental regulations were found to have a large direct effect.

Nevertheless, we must still be guarded in drawing conclusions about the total macroeconomic impacts of federal environmental regulations. There are at least two (and perhaps more) ways in which regulation can affect the economy that are not reflected in the studies discussed here and that may never adequately be incorporated in such studies.

The first concerns the potentially inflationary effects of environmental regulation. As discussed above, the models generate these effects as the higher operating costs resulting from regulation are passed on in the form of higher prices for intermediate and final products. But if the "catch-up" phenomenon Barry Bosworth describes is pervasive—if workers are successful in recouping in higher wages the price increases resulting from regulation—then environmental regulation will have indirect effects not adequately reflected in most models.

There is another, even more important, indirect macroeconomic

---

18. For example, Chase found unemployment higher throughout its simulation period in the "with-controls" case, while DRI found pollution control spending reduced the unemployment rate in its study. This may be because DRI took into account the jobs created in operating and maintaining pollution control equipment, while Chase appears to have ignored these employment effects in its 1972 study.

effect of environmental regulation that conventional models seem to be unable to capture. It, too, diminishes considerably any confidence we can place in the results of simulation studies. Regulation not only increases the costs of the governmental and industrial activities that are undertaken in the economy, it can also influence the decision whether or not to undertake them. Thus, applying stricter discharge standards to new sources than to existing ones may not only increase environmental expenditures by any new sources, it may also affect the number of new sources. Complicated environmental permitting procedures or requirements for preconstruction modeling of air quality may not only delay the construction of new plants, but also tip the balance against building certain of them at all.[19] The possibility that current regulations will be tightened or reinterpreted in the future may also inhibit new economic development.

These and other possible indirect effects of regulation share a common characteristic: it is virtually impossible to reflect them in a model of macroeconomic activity in any but a crude and ad hoc way. That is, no simple adjustments in parameter values will capture these effects, nor will shifts in any of the variables exogenous to the models. We suspect that such indirect effects will influence the level and location of industrial production, the rate at which new technologies are introduced (and, hence, productivity is augmented), the competitiveness of certain domestic markets, and other important characteristics of the economy as well. But we must be left to speculate as to the magnitude and timing of these effects. In view of this, it is wrong to vest too much importance in the quantitative results of the current vintage of macroeconomic simulation studies.

There is another reason to avoid literal interpretation of the results of macroeconomic analyses. Even if regulations that are gradually introduced could influence the level as well as the composition of employment and output, offsetting fiscal and monetary policy might negate these effects and produce others. Suppose, in other words, that any increase in unemployment automatically triggered increased government spending or other economic stimulation. Unless this response is incorporated in the simulation experiments,[20] the model-

---

19. The possibly deleterious consequences of new source performance standards and permitting delays are discussed by Harrington and Krupnick in this volume.

20. This has been attempted in the past. In the 1972 Chase study, for example, an additional simulation was run in which fiscal and monetary policy were used to keep real output and employment at the levels that would have existed in the no-controls case. Predictably, inflation was forecast to be somewhat higher when government policy was used to offset job loss. The 1978 DRI study also examined possible policy offsets. Included were runs in which policy attempted to hold interest rates constant, keep inflation to its level in the no-controls case, or keep real GNP constant.

ing results may indicate increased unemployment, even though the compensating policies triggered by such increases would lead to different effects altogether. The very real possibility of discretionary responses adds to the difficulty of the task described in this paper.

In view of the limitations discussed here, and those related to the expenditure data on which the macro studies are based, should we pay any attention to them at all? The answer is probably yes, if only because such studies will continue to be used to advance one side or another in the debate over environmental and other regulation. Several steps might be taken that could increase the usefulness of the resulting studies.

First, it would be preferable in future macroeconomic studies to enter a range of values for each of the expenditure estimates, rather than a point estimate. The range could vary from sector to sector, depending on the uncertainty of the estimate. For example, it could be specified that environmental expenditures in the petroleum refining industry in 1982 will be between $350 million and $600 million. If upper and lower bounds were entered for each value, the resulting output would give a broader but more honest picture of what we know of the likely effects of regulation. There is nothing unhelpful about a conclusion that current air and water pollution controls will add between 0.2 to 0.4 of 1 percentage point to the annual rate of inflation in 1984. Of course, a "most likely" or "average" value could be chosen where a range will not do, but the range should always be presented as a reminder of the uncertainty surrounding expenditure (and benefit) estimates, as well as the uncertainty inherent in macroeconomic modeling.

Second, an attempt should be made to incorporate at least some of the indirect effects of regulation in the modeling exercises. While difficult, at least one approach merits some consideration. The DRI model now includes a "sentiment" variable in the equations explaining consumer spending, which is designed to reflect optimism or pessimism about future economic conditions. It might be possible to construct a similar variable for "producer sentiment" that reflects in part expectations about additional future regulation or changes in existing rules. Such a variable might prove useful in helping explain business investment in new plant and equipment. If so, it could also help measure any potentially adverse effects of regulation on the economy, effects which have little or nothing to do with direct increases in production costs.

A final recommendation has to do with the benefits of environmental regulation. All the attention given to expenditure estimates (and, occasionally, cost estimates) has tended to obscure an important fact: while they are very difficult to estimate, the benefits of air and water pollution control are no doubt considerable. Moreover, while certain of these benefits are not reflected in the national income accounts,[21] other benefits might well influence gross national product. Thus, although the beneficial effects of regulation have not been included in past studies, they should be included in future efforts to determine the macroeconomic effects of environmental regulation.

This is not the place to review the benefits of environmental regulation. Freeman has recently done that elsewhere.[22] He has also suggested which portions of the likely benefits of air and water pollution control will affect gross national product and which will not.[23] According to Freeman, of the $21.4 billion in benefits that may have arisen in 1978 as a result of air quality improvements in the United States since 1970, $19.8 billion could be considered "utility-increasing" benefits, while $1.6 billion could be termed "cost-reducing or output-increasing." The utility-increasing benefits include outputs of regulation for which people would be willing but do not have to pay—and which, therefore, do not show up in market transactions. These include enhanced amenities arising from improved air quality and reductions in the risk of illness or death related to air pollution. The cost-reducing or output-increasing benefits take the form of enhanced agricultural yields, reduced medical costs, reductions in household cleaning costs, and reductions in materials damage caused by pollution. With respect to water pollution control, utility-increasing benefits include enhanced recreational opportunities and increased amenity values; cost-reducing benefits include lower treatment costs to municipalities and industries using intake waters; and output-increasing benefits include those from commercial fisheries.

At the very least, the cost-reducing and output-increasing benefits of air and water pollution control should be included in future simulation studies. This should not be too difficult to do. For example, reduced spending on health care or household cleaning could easily be accommodated in an econometric model, as could reductions in industrial costs resulting from cleaner water or air.

One such adjustment could significantly affect the results of the

---

21. For a discussion of omissions from the national income and product accounts, *see* Peskin's paper in this volume.

22. *See* A. Freeman, The Benefits of Air and Water Pollution Control: A Review and Synthesis of Recent Evidence (December 1979) (report prepared for the U.S. Council on Environmental Quality, Washington, D.C.).

23. *See* A. Freeman, Benefits of Pollution Control: Review and Synthesis (1979) (unpublished manuscript based on A. Freeman, *supra* note 22).

simulation studies. If air pollution does have the effect on sickness and lost productivity that some have estimated it might,[24] improved air quality could be reflected in the econometric models by increases in labor productivity. This might substantially affect the inflation and unemployment rates predicted by the models, as well as future trends in real output and other important variables. Even if adjustments like these are made, the models will still not be able to reflect the utility-increasing benefits of pollution control. Some of them will never be reflected in market transactions, and hence will not be amenable to simulation.

An observation is in order about including regulatory benefits in future simulations: the results may be surprising to some. Suppose, for example, as a result of regulation and improved environmental quality, less money is spent on health, cleaning, and other "defensive" expenditures. Then the unemployment rate predicted by an econometric model may be higher during part or all of the simulation period than if these beneficial effects had not been included. Similarly, increased labor productivity resulting from clean air might mean that fewer workers are required to produce a given output than before. This, too, might manifest itself in the form of increased unemployment.

On the other hand, the inflation rate may be lower in the "with-benefits" scenario than without. Less spending, coupled with decreased costs to manufacturers, would probably mean lower prices. Depending on the way that benefits are entered into the simulation models, other effects will no doubt appear. While it is difficult to guess their direction, some will influence certain variables in the "wrong" way—e.g., more inflation, higher unemployment, a less favorable balance of trade, and so on. Just because benefits are the favorable result of regulation, it does not follow that their macroeconomic manifestation will be favorable. This should not be surprising since the expenditures (or costs) associated with regulation appear to have some favorable macroeconomic effects.

AUTHOR'S NOTE

As this volume went to press, EPA announced the results of a 1981 update of DRI's 1978 macroeconomic analysis.[25] This update dif-

---

24. T. Crocker, et al., *Methods Development for Assessing Air Pollution Control Benefits*, in U.S. ENVT'L PROTECTION AGENCY, 1 EXPERIMENTS IN THE ECONOMICS OF EPIDEMIOLOGY (1979).

25. Data Resources Incorporated, "The Macroeconomic Impact of Federal Pollution Control Programs: 1981 Assessment," prepared for the Environmental Protection Agency, July 1981.

fered from the 1978 DRI study in several respects. First, the cost estimates upon which the 1981 simulations were based were higher than those used in the 1978 study. For the first time the estimates included projected spending in response to solid and hazardous waste regulations and regulations governing toxic substance control, as well as expenditures expected to arise as a result of the 1977 amendments to the Clean Air Act and Clean Water Act. In addition, the 1981 update used a newer version of the DRI model.

In spite of these differences, there were no major qualitative changes in the results. According to DRI, compliance with environmental regulation is still predicted to exacerbate inflation, reduce the rate of growth of productivity and real income, and stimulate employment throughout the simulation period (1970–87). Because the 1981 update assumed higher compliance costs, however, the size of these effects has changed from the 1978 study. For instance, in the 1981 study DRI predicted that environmental regulation would increase the average annual inflation rate between 1970 and 1987 by 0.4 percentage points (as opposed to 0.25 in the 1978 study). Between 1981 and 1987, according to the 1981 DRI study, environmental regulation will add nearly 0.6 percentage points to the annual inflation rate. This is a substantially higher effect than predicted in the 1978 analysis.

DRI estimated that the average annual rate of growth of real GNP would be slowed by about 0.1 of a percentage point, as a result of environmental regulation, as would the annual rate of productivity growth. DRI predicted in their 1981 update that environmental regulation would reduce the unemployment rate by 0.4 percentage points, a finding consistent with their 1978 analysis.

APPENDIX
ESTIMATING FORGONE CONSUMERS' SURPLUS

It was noted earlier that expenditures on pollution control are not necessarily the same as the social or opportunity costs of pollution control. In general, the latter will exceed the former because expenditure data do not reflect the forgone surpluses resulting from regulation or any costs arising from delay, uncertainty, locational, or other effects of environmental regulation on economic activity.[26]

It is possible to make a very rough estimate for a particular industry of the forgone consumers' surplus that may result from environ-

---

26. Other authors have made similar points. *See* R. Crandall, A Review of EPA Industry Cost Studies (paper presented for the National Commission on Air Quality) and R. Leone & D. Garvin, Regulatory Cost Analysis: An Overview (1980) (paper prepared for the National Commission on Air Quality).

mental regulation. This cost of regulation can be illustrated diagrammatically as in Figure 1. There the demand for a product is represented by the downward sloping line DD^1. For simplicity, assume the product can be produced at constant cost OP_1, so that supply is assumed to be perfectly elastic at this price. As the figure indicates, at price P_1, OA units of the product are sold.

FIGURE 1

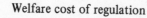

Welfare cost of regulation

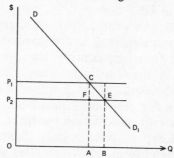

However, the cost of production of the good—and hence its price, OP_1—includes the effects of environmental regulation on the producer. Without these regulations and the expenditures they necessitate, a lower price—say OP_2—could be charged for the product in question. This would not only eliminate direct pollution control expenditures equal to $P_1 P_2 DC$ (which would be included in expenditure surveys), it would also reduce another cost. This is represented by the triangle CDE. It is the consumers' surplus that would be enjoyed on the additional units that would be purchased at price OP_2 (or that is forgone because of regulation). If we let ϵ represent the elasticity of demand for the good in question, the lost consumers' surplus associated with regulation, which we call ΔW, may be approximated by:

$$\Delta W = \frac{\epsilon (OP_1 - OP_2)^2 \, OA}{2 OP_1} \tag{1}$$

Now, suppose the units in question are new automobiles. According to EPA, the cumulative effect of all proposed vehicle emissions controls for carbon monoxide, hydrocarbons, and nitrogen oxides would add slightly more than $500 to the average sticker price of a 1981 model year car.[27] This is the expression $(OP_1 - OP_2)$ in Equa-

27. According to Putnam, Hayes and Bartlett, Inc., the cumulative effect of all controls on sticker prices of 1981 cars is $435 in 1977 dollars ("Comparisons of Estimated and Actual Pollution Control Cost for Selected Industries," prepared for the Office of Planning

tion (1). If the average sticker price of a 1981 model year car is $8,000, and if 9 million new 1981 cars are sold, the welfare loss associated with emissions controls can be calculated by substituting these numbers and a value for ϵ, the elasticity of demand and solving (1). According to Burright and Enns,[28] the elasticity of demand for new cars is approximately 0.7. Hence,

$$\Delta W = \frac{(0.7)(\$500)^2 (9 \times 10)^6}{\$16,000}$$

or about $98 million in 1979 dollars.

Two observations are in order. First, this very rough estimate of forgone consumer surplus is small in comparison with the direct expenditures on vehicle emissions controls that would show up in surveys. For example, in the illustrative case considered here, direct expenditures would be equal to $4.5 billion (9 million cars times $500 in expenditures for emission control per car).[29] In this case, then, one part of the cost of pollution control that goes unmeasured by pollution control expenditures is only slightly more than 2 percent of measured expenditures. Moreover, this estimate may be high because of the emissions control waivers that EPA has granted several of the automakers. These waivers have reduced the actual cost of complying with the emission standards below the figure used here.

Of course, this very rough estimate of $98 million represents an unmeasured cost of regulation for a single, although admittedly important, product. If similar calculations of consumer surplus loss could be made for all final products, the total would surely run into the billions. Moreover, the $500 price differential represents only the cost of the vehicle emissions controls. It does not include the effect of the other expenditures automakers must make to ensure that car production takes place in an environmentally sound way. Nor does the differential include the cost of the safety features and equipment required by federal regulations.[30]

---

and Evaluation, U.S. Environmental Protection Agency, February 1980, Table 13, Column 7). This was converted to 1979 dollars using the implicit price deflator for new plant and equipment control.

28. B. Burright & J. Enns, *Econometric Models of the Demand for Motor Fuel* (April 1975) (Rand Corporation Report No. R-1561-NSF/FEA).

29. As Table 3 indicates, CEQ's estimate of 1979 expenditures on mobile source pollution control is considerably higher than this. This is because the CEQ estimate also includes a fuel economy penalty resulting from emission control devices, as well as expenditures for maintenance and replacement of the catalyst in some pollution control equipment.

30. The estimate may be low for another reason, too. If autos cannot be produced at constant marginal cost as assumed in the example, there will also be a producers' surplus generated in production. Thus, by increasing production cost, environmental regulation reduces not only consumers' but also producers' surpluses. *See* R. Leone & D. Garvin, *supra* note 25, at 9–13.

Environmental Regulations and Productivity Growth

ROBERT H. HAVEMAN and GREGORY B. CHRISTAINSEN*

One of the primary mysteries of economic performance in the 1970s has been the slowdown in the rate of productivity growth—and an even more serious absolute reduction in productivity in the later years of the decade. As Barry Bosworth points out in this volume, this decline in productivity reflects a fundamental problem in macroeconomic performance, and underlies other symptoms of economic malfunction. For example, accelerating inflation rates may well generate inefficiencies in the economy which contribute to a decline in productivity growth. Conversely, to the extent that deficiencies in the aggregate supply of output relative to aggregate demand create inflationary pressures, low rates of productivity growth may contribute to these pressures. Stagflation and declining rates of productivity growth are part of the same phenomenon.

Many causes have been suggested for stagflation and declining productivity growth, including increased energy prices, a slowdown in capital investment, changing composition of outputs (from high to low productivity growth industries), changing composition of the labor force (from prime-age males toward youths and females, both with relatively short histories of labor market activity), a decline in the nation's work ethic, and regulatory activities—in particular environmental regulations.

The first section of this paper discusses the concept and measurement of productivity growth and its performance over the past several years. In the second section, the main hypotheses concerning the recent slowdown in this indicator of economic performance are identified. The third section examines one of these hypotheses: that governmental regulations are responsible for slowing down productivity growth. In particular, it identifies the channels by which regulations,

*Robert H. Haveman is a professor in the Department of Economics and a fellow of the Institute for Research on Poverty at the University of Wisconsin, Madison. Gregory Christainsen is an assistant professor in the Department of Economics at Colby College, Waterville, Maine. Some sections of the paper rely on G. Christainsen, F. Gollop, & R. Haveman, Environmental and Health-Safety Regulations, Productivity Growth, and Economic Performance: An Assessment (1980) (report prepared for the Office of Technology Assessment of the Joint Economic Committee of the United States Congress) and G. Christainsen & R. Haveman, *Public Regulations and the Slowdown in Productivity Growth*, 71 AM. ECON. REV. 320 (May 1981).

especially environmental regulations, could affect productivity growth. The fourth section estimates the impact of these policies on the manufacturing sector.

Numerous other efforts to identify how environmental regulations contribute to the slowdown in productivity growth are discussed in the fifth section. Finally, an estimate or "guestimate" is made of the role environmental regulations play in this slowdown in productivity growth.

INDEXES OF PRODUCTIVITY AND THEIR RECENT PERFORMANCE

Economic performance is gauged by statistical indicators that reflect changes in both output (e.g., changes in gross national product) and inputs (e.g., unemployment rates, labor force growth rates, and rates of capacity utilization). However, only one indicator—productivity—simultaneously captures both aspects of economic performance.

Theoretically, a nation's productivity can be defined simply as its aggregate final output per unit of input. However, because of the diversity in both outputs and inputs, this measurement is not a straightforward matter. The most common procedure is to measure productivity by obtaining an estimate of final aggregate private sector output divided by the number of worker-hours of labor input used to produce this output. This results in a single-factor productivity measure; it does not reflect in its denominator the full set of inputs. Because of this weakness, efforts have been made to construct more comprehensive productivity indicators—for example, private sector output per total factor input.[1]

Irrespective of the indicator employed, productivity performance in the 1970s has been far weaker than in the 1960s. For example, between 1965 and 1975, labor productivity grew at a rate of 2.2 percent per year, compared with a 3.4 percent annual rate of growth over the two preceding decades. Beginning in 1973, a further falloff occurred, and between 1973 and 1978 the annual growth rate of productivity barely exceeded 1 percent. In both 1979 and 1980, productivity not only failed to grow, but actually declined. A similar picture emerges if productivity indicators other than labor productivity are observed. Indeed, using any of the indicators, if the productivity

---

1. *See, e.g.,* J. KENDRICK, POST-WAR PRODUCTIVITY TRENDS IN THE UNITED STATES: 1948–1969 (1973); E. DENISON, ACCOUNTING FOR SLOWER ECONOMIC GROWTH (1979); and F. Gollop & D. Jorgenson, *United States Factor Productivity by Industry, 1947–1973,* in NEW DEVELOPMENTS IN PRODUCTIVITY MEASUREMENT AND ANALYSIS (J. Kendrick & B. Vaccara eds. 1980).

growth trend of the 1950s and 1960s had continued through the 1970s, the average productivity of the economy at the end of the decade would have been at least 15 percent above the level actually attained.

If one delves below the aggregate indexes of productivity growth, substantial disparity among sectors can be seen. For example, in the manufacturing sector, the slowdown was marked but relatively mild. In 1979, when overall productivity fell, manufacturing productivity grew by 1.8 percent. In the nonmanufacturing sectors, growth slowed most noticeably in the mining, construction, and electric utility industries. In fact, a major share of the overall productivity slowdown is attributable to the poor performance of these industries.[2]

POSSIBLE CAUSES OF REDUCED PRODUCTIVITY GROWTH

Numerous reasons have been put forward to explain the deceleration in productivity growth. A few of these factors are briefly discussed.

Composition of Output

There have been two major sectoral shifts in the composition of output in recent decades. The first shift is from the farm to the nonfarm sector. Second, within the nonfarm sector, output has shifted away from manufactured goods toward services.

Because the level of labor productivity in the farm sector has on average been much lower than that for nonfarm labor, the shift of output from farm to nonfarm sectors has contributed to the overall rise in labor productivity since World War II. However, most of this shift occurred before 1966; since 1967, very little additional movement has taken place. Moreover, levels of labor productivity in the farm and nonfarm sectors are now much closer than they were two decades ago. Therefore, one of the major sources of productivity growth in the two decades after the war no longer existed in the 1970s.

The second shift—from production of manufactured goods to services—has contributed to the slowdown in the nonfarm private business sector. The relative share of manufacturing in total employment has been decining steadily for two decades. Because the opportunity for introducing mass production techniques or achieving economies of scale are relatively limited in the service sector, productivity is below that in manufacturing and has tended to grow more slowly as

---

2. The preceding statistical information is derived from E. DENISON, *supra* note 1.

well. As a result, the shift away from manufacturing and toward services has tended to reduce overall productivity growth.

Advances in Knowledge and Research and Development (R&D)

Advances in knowledge can enhance productivity in either of two ways. They can directly enhance the quality of inputs (e.g., better educated workers), or they may enable producers to combine inputs of existing quality in a more efficient manner. As a percentage of gross national product, R&D spending reached a peak in the mid-1960s during the high-water years of the nation's space effort. At that time R&D accounted for roughly 3 percent of the gross national product. Since 1966, however, R&D has undergone a slow decline until it now accounts for only about 2 percent of the gross national product.[3]

Composition of the Labor Force

The changing demographic nature of the nation's work force has been postulated as a cause of the decline in productivity growth. Since 1966 there have been sharp increases in the labor force and in labor force participation rates, and the age-sex composition of these increases has been heavily weighted toward women and teenagers. Because these groups have modest amounts of work experience and job training, they are typically less productive than their more experienced counterparts. This is most apparent in the case of teenagers. In the case of women, there have been barriers to the more productive lines of work, irrespective of age, and women have also had relatively fewer opportunities for training. This expansion in the less skilled portion of the labor force may be reducing the average growth rate of labor productivity. Of course, as these workers develop skills, they will contribute to productivity growth.

Capital-Labor Ratio

The level of investment in the economy and, in turn, the capital-labor ratio are important in achieving increases in productivity. It is largely through new plant and equipment that more advanced technologies are introduced into the production process. Moreover, in the absence of increases in capital inputs, producers will experience diminishing marginal returns for each additional unit of labor employed.

At the same time that the labor force in the United States has increased its growth rate, the country's capital stock has grown at a

---

3. NATIONAL SCIENCE FOUNDATION, SCIENCE INDICATORS (1979).

somewhat reduced rate. Net of depreciation, capital per employed person rose at an average annual rate of about 2.0 percent from 1948 to 1969, but between 1969 and the present, the annual rate of growth fell to about 1.2 percent.[4]

Energy Prices

For many years, the United States enjoyed the availability of cheap energy. The increases in the world price of crude oil by the OPEC cartel that began in 1973 have undoubtedly seriously affected productivity and economic performance in a number of industrialized Western nations.

While changes in relative prices occur daily without tremendous strain to the economic system, the magnitude of the energy price change, combined with the complementary nature of energy and capital, was a serious blow. The sharp hike in energy prices increased the obsolescence of much of the capital already invested. Plant and equipment intended to be used for years suddenly became less profitable to employ. Moreover, businesses faced adjustment costs in learning how to operate in the new energy price environment, and in making necessary changes in the structure of production.

Other Factors

Several other factors have been cited as possible causes of the slowdown in productivity growth: disincentive effects of income taxes, disruption of expectations brought about by rapidly changing rates of inflation, and negative attitudes toward work are some examples. In general, however, investigations to date have relegated these factors to a minor role. The factors we have discussed here, plus government regulations, are thought to have been among the more decisive ones.

GOVERNMENT REGULATIONS AS A SOURCE OF THE PRODUCTIVITY SLOWDOWN

By definition, government regulations are interventions into market processes. They alter the utility and profit-maximixing decisions of individual decision makers. In a smoothly functioning market economy (without externalities such as pollution), such interventions will cause the private sector production levels to deviate from those which could have been attained without intervention. Holding output composition constant, this deviation means that additional inputs are

---

4. *See* E. DENISON, *supra* note 1, at 52.

required to reach any given level of output. Under these conditions, *increases* in government regulation will be associated with *larger deviations* from the potential level of private output, and equivalently, reduced rates of growth of output per unit of input—in other words, decreases in productivity.

The channels by which government regulations are likely to affect either the output (numerator) or input (denominator) of productivity indexes are complex. A discussion of environmental regulations illustrates these channels.

Over the past several years, government regulations have required that increasing amounts of labor and capital be devoted to pollution abatement. While such mandated investments may generate substantial benefits, their contribution to the output of marketed goods and services produced is minimal. In the mid-1970s, capital spending stood at about 9.5 percent of gross national product. This figure drops to 8.7 percent if one considers the investments mandated by these regulations to be nonproductive. If adapting to these regulations causes inputs to be employed which make little contribution to *measured* output, then *measured* productivity suffers on this account.[5]

The hypothesis that environmental regulations cause reductions in productivity growth is based on several conjectures. If environmental regulations cause businesses to increase labor input with no corresponding increase in output, or conversely, decrease output with no corresponding change in labor input, their effect will be to decrease productivity growth. The following is a summary of business responses to environmental regulations which could lead to reduced productivity growth.

1. Pollution control regulations require investments in control equipment which compete with normal investments in productive plant and equipment, crowding out the latter to some unknown extent. Hence, labor has less capital than it would otherwise have, and as a result its output may be reduced.
2. Pollution control regulations tend to be engineering standards rather than performance standards and thus induce an inefficiently high level of capital investment and intensity.
3. In both water and air regulations, new sources of pollution are subjected to much more stringent standards than existing sources. This uneven treatment may cause businesses to retain existing—and lower productivity—plants and equipment in use longer than otherwise, and to delay the introduction of new capital and more advanced technology.

---

5. For a discussion of measured and unmeasured outputs in the national income accounts, *see* H. Peskin's paper in this volume.

4. Pollution control equipment, once installed, requires labor for its operation and maintenance. This labor input makes no contribution to salable output. The same is true for manpower required to comply with the paperwork and legal burdens of regulation.

5. To avoid plant closings and layoffs, environmental regulations are written and enforced more stringently for fast-growing than for slow-growing industries, and thus inhibit an important source of productivity increase. This may have been true for the electric utility industry, which had an excellent record of productivity growth until the early 1970s.

6. Efforts to avoid any deterioration of pristine areas—the "prevention of significant deterioration" (PSD) provision—has retarded plant construction or resulted in the choice of less productive locations for new plants.

In principle, the dislocations occurring through each of these channels could be measured. In practice, however, data do not exist to reliably quantify any one of them. However, this is not to say that no efforts have been made to blame environmental regulations for some of the post-1970 reduction in productivity growth.

Analogous channels exist for the possible effect of environmental regulations on prices. As we have emphasized, the relationship between outputs and inputs—productivity—has implications for the relationship between output and costs. As a result, factors that affect productivity are apt to affect prices as well.

The precise magnitude of the increases in production costs caused by environmental control efforts is open to debate, but is generally agreed to run in the tens of billions of dollars. The Council on Environmental Quality estimated that the annual private costs of water and stationary air quality control will be $31.5 billion by 1988 (in 1979 dollars).[6]

In considering any of the alleged effects of environmental regulation on prices, two important distinctions must be kept in mind. First, one must distinguish changes in *relative* prices from changes in the *general* level of prices. Environmental regulation may cause the price of a commodity heavily affected to increase relative to other prices, but without the spiralling effect Barry Bosworth describes in his paper, it does not necessarily follow that there will be a general rise in prices throughout the economy. Second, one-time increases in prices must be distinguished from *continuing* increases. The fact that the rate of inflation was higher during the 1970s than in the 1960s

---

6. *See* COUNCIL ON ENVT'L QUALITY, ELEVENTH ANNUAL REPORT (1980).

means not only that the price level became higher during the 1970s but that the *rate of increase* of the price level rose as well. While it is clear that environmental regulation could cause the relative prices of particular goods and services to increase on a one-time basis, it is not necessarily responsible for an increase in the general level of prices, let alone *a growth in the rate of increase* of this level.

ESTIMATES OF THE SLOWDOWN IN MANUFACTURING PRODUCTIVITY GROWTH

Given these conjectures, it would seem important to measure, where possible, the relationship between government regulatory activities and productivity growth in industries that have been heavily affected by them. However, because of the difficulty of obtaining data and serious deficiencies in those that can be obtained, it is not easy to make such estimates.

On a more aggregate level, it is possible to obtain a "first-cut" estimate of the contribution of federal regulations to the productivity slowdown in the manufacturing sector by using a straightforward time series regression model.[7] First, it is assumed that a definable set of production relationships underlies economic activity in this sector. These relationships relate the flow of output (Q) to the flow of total factor input (TFI). The function shifts over time in response to changes in relative factor prices, business cycle shocks, and to what could be called "regulatory intensity."

These production relationships can be estimated for the U.S. manufacturing sector from 1958 to 1977 using the quantities and proportions of total cost accounted for by labor, capital, energy, and materials, and price and quantity data pertaining to output. These inputs can be combined into a measure of TFI by using their respective shares in total cost as weights. Because of this comprehensive set of inputs, the effect of some factors often assigned responsibility for the productivity slowdown (e.g., energy prices) is accounted for in the TFI measure.

It is difficult to define the concept of "regulatory intensity," let alone quantify it. Here, the definition is based on the view that regulatory agencies distort private sector decisions which would, in general, maximize the rate of productivity growth. Three alternative measures of regulatory intensity were constructed and used for the analysis. The first is based on an estimate of the cumulative number

---

7. A complete description of this analysis is found in G. Christainsen & R. Haveman, *Public Regulations and the Slowdown in Productivity Growth*, 71 AM. ECON. REV. 320 (May 1981).

of "major" pieces of regulatory legislation in effect during any of the years in question.[8] The second and third indexes are based on the volume of real federal expenditures on regulatory activities for the years in question[9] and the number of full-time federal personnel engaged in regulatory activities. Though they are crude proxies for regulatory intensity, these indexes do provide a reasonable characterization of postwar trends in the regulation of the manufacturing sector. Table 1 shows the results of time series regression estimates of the contribution of public regulations to the slowdown in productivity growth.[10]

TABLE 1

CONTRIBUTIONS TO THE RATE OF GROWTH OF LABOR PRODUCTIVITY IN U.S. MANUFACTURING, 1958–77

Source	Contribution during: 1958-65	1965-73	1973-77
Regulatory intensity (R)	0 to −0.1	−0.1 to −0.3	−0.2 to −0.3
Time trend (T)	0.9 to 1.0	0.9 to 1.0	0.9 to 1.0
Cyclical adjustment (Q/Q*)	0 to 0.1	0	0 to −0.1
Unexplained	0.4 to 0.5	−0.1 to −0.2	−0.3 to −0.4
Growth in total factor productivity	1.4	0.6	0.3
Capital/labor ratio (K/L)	1.6	1.9	1.4
Average growth rate of *labor* productivity	3.0	2.5	1.7

8. Basic data on the number of major prices of regulatory legislation, both in the traditional areas and the newer environmental and social areas, are found in CENTER FOR THE STUDY OF AMERICAN BUSINESS, DIRECTORY OF FEDERAL AGENCIES (Formal Publication No. 31:1980). Our series is calculated from those data.

9. Ideally, one would wish to have a consistent time series of the net changes in average and marginal firm costs attributable to regulations, or even a time series of the incremental expenditures required of firms. See the paper by Paul Portney in this volume.

10. The equation estimated is as follows:

$$\ln(TFP) = \ln A + \alpha R + \beta T + \gamma \ln\left(\frac{Q}{Q*}\right) + \delta \ln\left(\frac{Q}{Q*}\right)_{-1} + U$$

where α, β, γ, and δ are parameters, TFP is total factor productivity [a measure that differs from labor productivity by a factor reflecting the ratio of nonlabor to labor inputs (K/L)], R is the regulatory intensity variable, T is an annual time variable, Q is actual manufacturing output, $Q*$ is a measure of the level of output which would have been produced in the absence of cyclical influences, U is a random error term, and A is a constant. This equation was estimated for the U.S. manufacturing sector from 1958 to 1977 using unpublished annual data (obtained from the U.S. Bureau of Labor Statistics) on the quantities and proportions of total cost accounted for by labor, capital, energy, and materials and price and quantity data pertaining to output. These measures were combined into a measure of total factor input using their shares in total costs as weights. This input measure was then used to calculate total factor productivity.

These results suggest that federal regulations are responsible for from 12 to 25 percent of the slowdown in the growth of labor productivity in U.S. manufacturing for 1973–77 compared with 1958–65.[11] Reductions in the ratio of nonlabor to labor inputs (K/L) are responsible for about 15 percent of the slowdown. The contribution of the average cyclical impact could fall anywhere in the 0–15 percent range. The portion of the slowdown in the rate of labor productivity growth attributed to a change in labor force composition, R&D expenditures, or sectoral output shifts is captured in the row labeled "unexplained." These are the factors not measured explicitly in the regression model. Their impact remains substantial.

CONTRIBUTION OF ENVIRONMENTAL REGULATIONS TO THE DECLINE IN PRODUCTIVITY GROWTH

On the basis of the results reported for the manufacturing sector, it is reasonable to suggest that between, say, 12 and 25 percent of the slowdown in productivity growth in the private sector of the economy between the early 1960s to the mid-1970s can be attributed to the entire bundle of federal regulations. The contribution of only those regulatory activities designed to secure an improved environment must, as a result, be assigned a smaller role. How much smaller, however, is an open question:

During the past decade, several researchers have attempted to sort out the contribution of environmental regulation among the numerous other causes of the productivity slowdown. Some of these studies have adopted a comprehensive accounting framework, requiring that the sum of the contributions of all factors explaining productivity growth not exceed 100 percent. Others have been more specific, emphasizing only environmental regulations or the performance of industries particularly affected by them. In this section, some of the more prominent studies dealing explicitly with the role of environmental regulations will be discussed and critiqued.

Perhaps the most comprehensive approach seeks to allocate the total decrease in productivity growth among a host of its determinants within a "growth accounting" framework. In this approach, typified by the work of Edward Denison,[12] separate estimates of the

11. As the table indicates, the growth rate of labor productivity in the 1958–65 period was 3 percent. By 1973–77, it had fallen to 1.7 percent, a decrease of 1.3 percentage points. Between the same two periods, the negative contribution of regulations (R) increased from 0 to −0.1 to −0.2 to −0.3. If one takes the estimate for the early period to be essentially zero, the range of the R contribution to the 1.3 percentage points is from 0.15 (0.2/1.3) to 0.23 (0.3/1.3). Hence, our 12–25 percent estimate.

12. E. DENISON, ACCOUNTING FOR UNITED STATES ECONOMIC GROWTH 1929–1969 (1974) and E. Denison, *Explanations of Declining Productivity Growth*, 59 SURVEY OF CURRENT BUS. 1 (Aug. 1979).

role played by various determinants are made, often on the basis of rough, ad hoc analyses, along with a good dose of judgment. Then the remaining, unaccounted-for residual is assigned to a broad, catch-all category. Denison measures productivity in terms of output (defined as final product in the national income and product accounts) per unit of factor input, and confines his analysis to the nonresidential business sector, where environmental regulation is concentrated. Output is valued at factor cost (including profits), and factor input is a combined measure of labor, capital, and land. Energy and materials inputs, not being primary input factors like labor and capital, are not explicitly and separately analyzed by Denison. Nonetheless, the aggregate measure of factor input which he uses is derived from the national income accounts. As a result, his overall estimates reflect these inputs as well as the primary factors which he analyzes.

Denison estimates the contribution of various determinants to productivity growth during the 1969–76 period relative to 1948–69. After adjusting his productivity data for what he terms "irregular factors"—weather, work stoppages, and cyclical factors—he considers changes in labor force characteristics, such as hours worked and age-sex composition. These factors had a negative impact on productivity growth during both pre- and post-1969 periods. By contrast, education had a positive impact in both periods.

The amount of capital and land with which the labor force works is the next major category Denison examines. The contribution of this factor to productivity growth over the years has declined only slightly. The movement of labor out of both agriculture and self-employment appears to have had a more significant effect, making a 0.4-percentage-point-per-year contribution to productivity during 1948–69, and none in 1973–76.

Denison then turns to the role of environmental regulations and measures the incremental costs in production resulting from these regulations. These costs are used to indicate the reduction in output attributable to regulation. This procedure, in effect, assumes that the factor inputs required for environmental control are diverted directly from marketed output, resulting in an equivalent decrease in the output numerator of the productivity index.

Although capital goods purchased by business for pollution abatement count as part of measured output, Denison reduces measured output by an amount equal to the value of the services this capital would have provided if it were used to produce final products instead of improved environmental quality. The value of these alternative outputs is treated in his analysis as an opportunity cost.

This net incremental cost estimate is then used to construct an index of the effect of post-1967 environmental regulations on productivity growth which shows that these regulations had no effect from 1948 to 1967, an average annual effect of 0.05 percentage point from 1967 to 1969, a 0.1 percentage point effect from 1969 to 1973, and a 0.22 percentage point effect from 1973 to 1975. In an update to his earlier study, Denison estimated the average annual reduction in productivity growth due to environmental regulation for 1975–78 to have fallen to 0.08 percentage point. Relative real expenditures on labor and capital mandated by the regulations had slowed down by this period.[13]

One of the striking aspects of the Denison study is the huge residual factor (which he labels "advances in knowledge and not elsewhere classified") with which he is left. This factor accounts for *over half* of the total 1948–69 productivity growth. For 1969–73, the residual figure of 1.6 percentage points per year equals the measured rate of productivity growth for that period. And for 1973–76, the residual factor suddenly drops to 0.7 percentage point per year, which is *greater* in absolute value than the –0.5 percentage point rate at which productivity fell during these years. Although Denison argues plausibly that advances in knowledge may have contributed less to recent growth, his study leaves unanswered the reasons for such a sudden decline in his residual category during the most recent period.

With respect to this mysterious change in the residual component, Denison's evaluation of the role of the post-1973 increase in energy prices takes on significance. In Denison's analysis, this factor is estimated to have contributed only 0.1–0.2 percentage point annually to the productivity decline. This approach, however, does not consider the long-run (dynamic) effects of the energy problem, which involve the costs of adapting plants to use substitute fuels and the increased obsolescence of some plant and equipment because of other factor substitutions. Denison's estimate also ignores the diversion of labor and capital to the redesign of products and retooling for production when energy prices induce a switch in the pattern of consumer demand (e.g., from large to small, fuel-efficient cars).[14]

Also troublesome are difficulties in capturing changes in technological advance. To some extent, technological change is embodied in physical capital, and its rate of change depends in part on the rate of change in the stock of physical capital. By the same token, Denison's estimate of the contribution of physical capital may be entangled

---

13. E. Denison, *Pollution Abatement Programs: Estimates of Their Effect upon Output per Unit of Input, 1975–78*, 59 SURVEY OF CURRENT BUS. 58 (Aug. 1979).

14. These effects have been emphasized in E. Hudson & D. Jorgenson, *Energy Prices and the U.S. Economy, 1972–1976*, 18 NAT. RES. J. 877 (1978).

with the contributions of technology and other factors which lower the real price of capital goods.

Denison's study, then, concludes that environmental regulations affect productivity negatively and have had an increasing effect, at least through 1974. But these regulations still appear to account for a relatively small portion of the measured productivity slowdown. The decrease in impact for the most recent period is noteworthy.

A second empirical approach to explaining the slowdown in productivity growth employs a time series macroeconomic methodology. While the growth accounting approach is rather ad hoc, this second approach relies on statistical estimates of the effect of various factors. The productivity time series is observed and breaks in the series are identified by statistical analysis. Then, using a regression framework, the determinants of the breaks are statistically estimated and the contribution of each is measured.

An important and recent example of this approach is contained in a study by Robin Siegel.[15] In this research, Siegel identified breaks in the series in both 1967 and 1973. In statistically explaining these breaks, change in the demographic composition of the labor force was found to be consistently important, while (from 1973 on) changes in relative energy prices were the single most important factor. Pollution abatement expenditures were a significant negative factor in the post-1967 slowdown, and continued to contribute to the productivity slowdown until 1975.

Output per worker hour in the private nonfarm sector served as the dependent variable for Siegel's regressions. In addition to those mentioned above, variables to control for cyclical factors, the share of manufacturing in total output, and the capital/output ratio were included in the regression. Even with the addition of these variables, there were statistically significant break points in 1967 and 1973.

Thus, Siegel's analysis does account for a large portion of the productivity slowdown, with energy prices being assigned a much more significant role than in Denison's analysis, but the sharpness of the decline and the breaks in trend remain unexplained. Siegel suggests looking at the age of the capital stock, additional government regulations, such as those in the health and safety area, and changes in attitudes toward work. In addition to these, variables to control for expenditures in education and training, research and development, along with changes in economies of scale should be employed. They have been significant in other studies and their omission in Siegel's

---

15. R. Siegel, *Why Has Productivity Slowed Down?*, DATA RES. U.S. REV. 1.59 (March 1979).

work may result in biased estimates of the effects of the included variables.

In the time series macroeconometric approach, the pattern of changes in aggregate productivity over time is studied in conjunction with the time pattern of other aggregate variables which might be expected to relate to, or explain, it. In this way, an association between productivity change and its determinants—say, regulatory intensity or cyclical change—can be established. An alternative approach is to study patterns of productivity change in individual industries. This can be done either over time within an industry or across industries at a point in time. Again, the effort is to see if high and low levels of change are associated with variations in the intensity of environmental regulations and other relevant independent variables.

Such microeconometric estimates have been made by Robert Crandall.[16] His first analysis involved a comparison over time of productivity growth in selected industries. He compared the primary "pollution-control impacted industries" in the 1958–73 period (before policy-induced pollution control expenditures really took their bite) with their performance in the post-1973 period. He found that the affected industries experienced productivity growth of about 5 percent per year prior to 1973, while manufacturing as a whole had a productivity growth rate of about 3 percent per year. After 1973, however, the situation reversed itself. While the rate of productivity growth in the total manufacturing sector fell to 1.4 percent, the rate in the sectors heavily affected by regulations fell to less than 1 percent. This simple comparison, of course, says nothing about the other forces affecting these industries which could also have contributed to a reduction in productivity. Changes in energy prices, investment levels, labor force composition, and the composition of intraindustry output come immediately to mind. It is not unreasonable to believe that industries affected by pollution control are also affected significantly by energy prices, cyclical changes, and other factors.

Crandall's second analysis employs a cross-section regression model (using 36 industries for which pollution control expenditures and productivity data are available) to explain the variance in productivity growth rates during the 1973–76 period. The dependent variable in Crandall's analysis is the deviation of an industry's productivity index from the forecast 1976 productivity, which was based on the histor-

---

16. R. Crandall, Is Environmental Policy Responsible for Declining Productivity Growth? (Dec. 28, 1979) (paper prepared for Annual Meeting of Society of Government Economists) and R. Crandall, *Pollution Controls and Productivity Growth in Basic Industries*, in PRODUCTIVITY MEASUREMENTS IN REGULATED INDUSTRIES (T. Cowing & R. Stevenson eds. 1980).

ical growth rate from 1958 to 1973. Of the numerous factors which could explain changes in productivity growth rates, only two variables are used: one to account for the effect of cyclical swings in output and the other to reflect pollution control costs. Crandall concludes that a 50 percent increase in pollution control costs over 1976 levels for the 36 industries would reduce productivity growth by 1.2 percentage points (or about one-third the average annual productivity growth). Also, if the results are extrapolated to all manufacturing, the 1976 reduction in productivity attributable to the bulk of pre-1976 pollution control expenditures would be 1.5 percentage points.

In his final analysis, Crandall estimated time series regressions for 10 heavily affected industries (plus electric utilities and all manufacturing) over 1954–76. The dependent variable was labor productivity and the independent variables were measures of the business cycle and a time trend. By examining the measured errors of the regression for each industry for the post-1970 period (or subperiods), Crandall sought to determine if there was a shortfall in productivity growth that was not accounted for by the independent variables. He concluded that in the industries affected by pollution control, productivity growth in the post-1970 period is less than in manufacturing as a whole, but that the difference was not substantial. Electric utilities had a substantial negative error in all post-1970 subperiods. The relatively small size of the negative impact of the highly regulated industries suggests that cyclical changes in output in the post-1970 period account for much of the productivity shortfall.

While Crandall's analysis is consistent with other studies suggesting a nontrivial role for environmental regulations in the recent productivity slowdown, his analyses are in no way definitive, as he clearly recognizes. The magnitude of the pollution control burden does appear to explain some of the shortfall in productivity performance in his cross-section analysis, and his extrapolated estimate of a 1.5 percentage point reduction in productivity growth as a result of environmental controls over a three-year period is higher than the impact suggested by Denison. Crandall's cross-section analysis controls only roughly for but one additional potential determinant of productivity declines during the 1973–76 period—cyclical swings in output. Hence, the effects of a host of other potential determinants of productivity change—the pattern of R&D spending, changes in energy prices, changes in labor force composition—are not accounted for and may seriously bias the results. Crandall's industry-specific time series analysis has much the same problem of omitted variables, as again only cyclical output swings (plus a time trend) are entered into the equation. The entire unexplained productivity shortfall is then attributed to pollution control regulations, even though a number of other potential determinants could just as well have contributed to it.

Crandall's microeconomic estimates, then, are rough and appear to attribute more of the productivity decrease to mandated environmental regulations than is warranted. If an implicit adjustment is made to his conclusions to account for the potential omitted variables, the effect of environmental regulations on productivity, while present, would appear to be rather small—substantially smaller than those suggested by Denison.

A final approach to estimating the effect of environmental regulations on productivity is through adoption of standard, intermediate-term, econometric models. With these models, the impact of aggregate expenditure or cost changes induced by environmental policy can be traced through the economy over time.[17]

The Data Resources macroeconomic study discussed by Portney indicates that environmental policy measures reduce productivity as the induced pollution control investment "crowds out" alternative capital investments in plant and equipment. In describing the results of their simulation analysis of labor productivity, DRI stated:

> The increased factor demands associated with the operating and maintenance and pollution abatement equipment resulted in a drop in labor productivity. Any given firm would now require additional employees to produce the same level of output. Further, the capital stock, which helps make the workers produce more, had been diluted with a portion which made no contribution to production. *The DRI model solution results indicate that productivity was 0.5% lower by 1978 and 1.4% lower in 1986, given the pollution requirements. Over the entire period, productivity growth averaged 0.1 percentage point a year less.* The reduction in productivity growth produces higher unit labor costs (the cost of labor associated with the production of a given unit of output). Initially these produce reduced profit margins, eroding corporate profits, but over time they get passed on in the form of higher prices.[18]

Table 2 shows the effect of pollution control policies on the annual labor productivity index over the 1970–86 period, as estimated by DRI. By the end of the seventeen-year period, the index of labor productivity was estimated to be 1.4 percentage points lower with than without the policy. However, by the end of the 1970–80 period, the productivity index with the controls was estimated to be only 0.3

---

17. This approach is discussed in detail in the paper by Portney in this volume.
18. Data Resources Inc., The Macroeconomic Impact of Federal Pollution Control Programs: 1978 Assessment (Jan. 29, 1979) (report submitted to the Environmental Protection Agency and the Council on Environmental Quality, Washington, D.C.).

TABLE 2

THE EFFECT OF POLICY-INDUCED POLLUTION CONTROL
EXPENDITURES ON THE LABOR PRODUCTIVITY INDEX, 1970–86,
IN PERCENTAGE POINTS

1970	+0.2	1979	−0.4
1971	+0.3	1980	−0.3
1972	+0.3	1981	−0.6
1973	+0.1	1982	−0.8
1974	−0.1	1983	−1.0
1975	−0.1	1984	−1.1
1976	−0.1	1985	−1.3
1977	−0.3	1986	−1.4
1978	−0.5		

Source: Supplemental data submitted to the Environmental Protection Agency by Data Resources Inc.

percentage point below that without the controls. Without the policy
in place, labor productivity was estimated to grow 42 percent over
the entire 1970–86 period; with the policy, the growth of labor productivity was estimated to be 39.9 percent.

The studies we have identified and described represent a wide
variety of analytical approaches to discerning the effect of environmental regulations on productivity. While each approach contributes
to a fuller understanding of the processes by which government regulations affect economic performance, each has its own special limitations and weaknesses.

Consider, first, the growth accounting analyses, as represented by
Denison. First, Denison implicitly assumes that, given the level of
total factor input, marketed output is crowded out by pollution-
control-mandated investments on a dollar-for-dollar basis. The decrease in final output which he attributes to pollution control regulations is based upon the output which would have been produced if
all mandated pollution abatement expenses had been, instead, expenditures on regular capital or labor and land devoted to producing
marketed output. Because of underemployed resources or factor substitution, however, output might not fall to the extent estimated by
Denison. In this respect, then, his estimate is likely to be higher than
the actual effect.

Second, Denison assumes no diminishing marginal rates of return
to additional expenditures on standard capital, labor, and land inputs.
This is done by attaching *average* rates of return estimates to the incremental standard inputs which would have been employed if they
had not been diverted by environmental regulations. If, as seems

likely, these additional inputs would have confronted diminishing marginal rates of return, their implicit contribution to output would have been less than Denison's estimates. Again, an upward-biased impact of environmental regulations is struck. On the other hand, Denison's estimates take no account of other, more subtle effects of regulation on productivity.

A clear strength of the growth accounting approach, however, is the comprehensiveness of its framework. The analyst is required to give recognition to the full set of factors which may be important in determining productivity growth—a requirement which a number of the more ad hoc or partial analyses do not fulfill. Having said this, however, it should be noted that Denison has been criticized for downplaying the effect of the post-1973 energy price increase on productivity growth.

The failure to consider relevant variables in the analysis is nowhere more clear than in the time series and microeconometric studies. All of these results remain open to question so long as potentially important variables, such as the age of the capital stock, expenditures on education, training, research and development, and changes in economies of scale are left out of the analysis. When the impacts of these variables are omitted, the estimated effects of the included variables are likely to be biased.

In defense of those who have attempted these time series and microeconometric studies, however, the serious data problems confronted should be emphasized. Some relevant aggregate time series data simply do not exist, and, at the industry level, important data (e.g., energy prices and usage and environmental or health/safety expenditures) are either unavailable or unreliable. Given these constraints, criticism of efforts which seek to do what one can with what is available should not be pushed too far.

The main strength of the macroeconomic models is their ability to capture a rather full set of behavioral relationships in a single framework. Moreover, only through these models can the problems of timing of impact be addressed. These strengths are offset by some notorious weaknesses. First, the underlying structure of the prominent models have been designed to yield short- and intermediate-term forecasts of the economy under various aggregate monetary and fiscal measures. When expenditures in a specific area (e.g., pollution control) are to be analyzed, the model is forced to treat them as generalized investment spending, with little recognition of their particular characteristics or impacts. Second, when adjustments have been made in the models in order to accommodate environmental policy measures, the adjustments have been crude and ad hoc. For this reason as well, the reliability of the estimates yielded by those models is open to question.

Two final points must be made with respect to all of the studies which have been undertaken to date. First, nearly all of them have taken, as the direct economic impact of regulations, estimates of the expenditures which these regulations have required. However, these data have serious weaknesses.[19] It is, for example, difficult to claim that these estimates across industries are likely to give a correct ordering of impact among them, let alone provide reasonable point estimates of resource requirements.

Finally, none of these studies has done justice to the role of regulations in creating an uncertain environment for business activity. Malkiel, for example, has emphasized the debilitating effect on investment and location decisions of regulations whose application and enforcement is problematic and unknown to the regulatee.[20] Similarly, Quarles has emphasized that clean air legislation, in particular, has led to serious delays and "stretch-outs" in investment plans, delays which have the inevitable effect of extending the use of outmoded facilities and retarding technical change and economic growth.[21] While these effects are difficult to model and estimate, their potential impact is nonetheless real.[22]

ENVIRONMENTAL REGULATIONS AND PRODUCTIVITY GROWTH–AN ASSESSMENT

This review of investigations of the causes of the post-1965 decline in productivity growth produces no clear-cut answers. It does, however, provide the basis for judging the contribution of environmental regulations to the decline. This assessment must, of course, consider

---

19. See Portney's discussion of these issues.

20. B. Malkiel, *Productivity–the Problem Behind the Headlines,* 57 HARV. BUS. REV. 81 (May-June 1979).

21. J. Quarles, *Federal Regulation of New Industrial Plants,* 10 ENVT'L RPTR. (BNA) (Monograph No. 28: May 4, 1979).

22. In addition to the few studies discussed here, a number of other studies have also attempted to assess the role of regulations and other factors in accounting for the slowdown in productivity growth. *See, e.g.,* Special Study on Economic Change (Part 2): Hearings Before the Joint Congressional Economic Committee, 95th Cong., 2d Sess. 476-87 (1978) (statement of Jerome A. Mark); *id.* at 596-616 (statement of Michael K. Evans); *id.* at 616-36 (statement of John W. Kendrick). *See also* J. Norsworthy, M. Harper, & K. Kunze, *The Slowdown in Productivity Growth: Analysis of Some Contributing Factors,* in 2 BROOKINGS PAPER ON ECONOMIC ACTIVITY 387 (Brookings Inst. ed. 1979) and L. Thurow, *The Productivity Problem,* 83 TECH. REV. 40 (Nov./Dec. 1980). These studies are reviewed and critiqued in G. Christainsen, F. Gollop, & R. Haveman, Environmental and Health-Safety Regulations, Productivity Growth, and Economic Performance: An Assessment (1980) (report prepared for the Office of Technology Assessment of the Joint Economic Committee of the United States Congress).

the role of environmental regulations in the context of a large number of other contributing factors and is admittedly tentative.

The changing demographic composition of the labor force and hours worked, together with sectoral shifts in the composition of output, appear to account for 20–30 percent of the slowdown in productivity. The slowdown in the rate of capital investment—resulting in a declining capital-labor ratio and a capital stock that embodies a technology which increasingly deviates from what is possible—should be credited with 25–30 percent of the slowdown.[23] A third important factor involves cyclical changes. The high unemployment and low utilization of the capital stock of the late 1960s and the 1970s, together with weather and work stoppages, appear to account for another 10–20 percent of the productivity slowdown. Finally between 10 and 40 percent of the slowdown is caused by a large number of other determinants, of which environmental regulations are but one. Little evidence exists to suggest that as much as 15 percent of the overall slowdown can be attributed to these regulations. A reasonable estimate—but one resting on a good deal of judgment—is that 8 to 12 percent of the slowdown in productivity is attributable to environmental regulations.

This estimate, it should be emphasized, accounts for both the *direct* and the *indirect* effects of environmental regulations. As a result, it includes whatever effects environmental regulations have on capital investment and the capital-labor ratio.[24]

Clearly, there is a wide range of uncertainty in this estimate. The research from which it is drawn varies in methodology, data, and the time periods analyzed. Our estimate is an amalgam which tries to sort through these differences, and to filter out the total effect of environmental regulations. In this vein, it should be noted that the evidence for an adverse impact of environmental regulations on the capital stock and its productivity is very weak. While the requirements of environmental policy could have major adverse effects on output

---

23. It should be noted that many analysts have included the potential effect of the post-1973 energy price increase in this capital determinant. This procedure presumes that the energy price increase reduced both investment and the return (productivity) to existing capital, and hence reduces the capital-labor ratio. Perhaps one-third to one-half of the 25–40 percent role assigned to the capital factor is attributable to the energy price increase.

24. *See* B. Fraumeni and D. Jorgenson, The Sectoral Sources of Aggregate U.S. Economic Growth 1948–1976 (1979) (unpublished report); B. Bosworth, *The Issue of Capital Shortages,* in CONG. JOINT ECON. COMM., 94TH CONG., 2D SESS., U.S. ECONOMIC GROWTH FROM 1976 TO 1986: PROSPECTS, PROBLEMS, AND PATTERNS (VOL. 3: CAPITAL) 1 (Comm. Print 1976); R. Eisner, *The Corporate Role in Financing Future Investment Needs, id.* at 16; and G. Christainsen, F. Gollop & R. Haveman, Environmental and Health-Safety Regulations, Productivity Growth, and Economic Performance: An Assessment (1980) (report prepared for the Office of Technology Assessment, U.S. Congress).

and productivity in certain sectors or industries, these effects tend to be localized. The sectors affected are small relative to the national economy, and reduced capital investment in them has a small effect on aggregate investment. Although both the direct and indirect effects of environmental regulation have been considered, some potential indirect effects may have been underestimated. For example, the rate of investment may have been depressed because of *uncertainties* caused by environmental regulations. This channel of impact was not explicitly considered.

One basic and overriding point should be made with respect to environmental regulations. The contributions to economic welfare which they are intended to make are, by and large, not reflected in measured output. These effects include improved health (implying less demand for medical care services), longer lives, expanded outdoor recreation opportunities, greater enjoyment of existing recreation opportunities, and reduced demands for cleaning and other "defensive" activities. If the standard productivity measures were effective indicators of economic welfare, these outputs would be included in the numerator of the measure.[25] Although they are difficult to quantify, let alone to value, numerous studies have indicated that marked increases in these social benefits have resulted from environmental policy. If this is in fact the case, the effect of these regulations on "true" productivity would be less negative than that estimated here—or even positive.

---

25. On this point, see H. Peskin's paper.

National Income Accounts
and the Environment
HENRY M. PESKIN*

INTRODUCTION

Recent declines in the gross national product (GNP) growth rate and associated measures of the nation's economic performance have caused public concern. Such concern is understandable because many individuals automatically associate material well-being with social well-being—a human failing existing at least from biblical times. Few professional economists would claim, however, that any economic indicator actually measures social well-being. Even the noneconomist knows that there has to be more to life than a large GNP.

The GNP and other measures of economic performance such as the net national product (NNP) and the national income (NI) are aggregations of entries in the nation's official income and product accounts. These are prepared by the Bureau of Economic Analysis in the Department of Commerce using data from the Census Bureau and many other public and private sources. While there is probably general agreement that these measures fail to reflect many facets of social well-being, they do indicate to a large degree what society does care about. Just how accurately they do this is a matter of debate.

The debate takes several forms and covers many related issues. A current version centers on the relationship between economic growth and the burdens environmental regulations place on industry, households, and government. The issue is whether the gains to society expected from the regulation—gains which generally do not show up in GNP—are being more than offset by losses in GNP precipitated by the regulations. This debate thus moves from the general question of how much of the "lost GNP" represents a loss in social well-being to the more specific one of how well the GNP reflects environmental change.

This paper addresses these issues by considering the following questions:

To what extent are changes in quality of the environment already appropriately measured by the GNP?

---

*Henry M. Peskin is a senior fellow in the Quality of the Environment Division, Resources for the Future.

Is it feasible to modify conventionally measured GNP so that it can more accurately account for environmental change?

Is it desirable to do so?

TO WHAT EXTENT DOES GNP CURRENTLY MEASURE CHANGES IN THE ENVIRONMENT?

Gross national product is a measure of the nation's annual production of goods and services. Given the narrowness of this definition, it is understandable to question how it is possible for an index of production to measure well-being in general or changes in the environment in particular. However, the production being measured consists of goods and services that do have some relation to the environment. About 63 percent of GNP is accounted for by the production of consumption goods, 17 percent by the production of investment goods (that is, heavy machinery, new plants, and so forth), and the remainder is largely governmental services.

Since it is likely that changes in both the physical environment and environmental policy responses will affect consumption and investment decisions as well as governmental activity, we can expect these changes to be reflected by some changes in the GNP. The trouble is that the size, or more important, the direction of the resulting changes in GNP are not obvious. If a rising GNP is associated with a "better life," then presumably GNP should fall as environmental quality decreases, all other things being equal. Similarly, GNP should rise in response to successful efforts to clean up the environment. Whether a rise or fall occurs depends on a host of factors that are masked by the GNP statistic.

Historically, periods of rapid industrialization have been associated with declines in air and water quality. Before concluding that a rise in GNP *necessarily* implies a deteriorating physical environment, it is necessary to look closely at the composition of the goods and services produced as the GNP changes. For example, if the service sector of the economy (insurance, legal, medical, other professional services) accounts for a large portion of the increase in GNP, as has been the case in recent years, air and water degradation may be minimal.

Of course, if a portion of the increase in GNP consists of goods consumed in order to "defend" against environmental degradation, then such consumption could be taken as evidence that the quality of the environment has declined. While such goods as paint, air filters, detergents, and health services could be purchased for such "defensive" purposes, it is not clear that was indeed the purpose of the purchase. Similarly, the increase in health services in recent years could be a sign of a wealthy society rather than a polluted one. In short, the problem is to separate "defensive" from ordinary expenditures.

Besides looking at the composition of goods embodied in an increased GNP, it may also be necessary to consider the composition of increases in pollutants before drawing conclusions on the amount of environmental degradation associated with an increase in GNP. Some pollutants are worse than others and increased emissions of some pollutants may have been offset by a decrease in others that are more obnoxious. As serious as automobile pollution may be, health problems associated with the more organic form of horsepower used in the 19th century may have been far worse.

Before concluding that environmental degradation and GNP increases are necessarily associated, we should consider the feedback effect of a poor physical environment on the ability to produce. A dirty environment can affect, not only the health of the work force and thus the productivity of labor, but also the productivity of capital equipment. For example, factories on Lake Erie and Lake Ontario report their water intake pipes clogged by algae, whose excessive growth is due to nutrient pollutants such as phosphorus and nitrogen compounds.[1]

We turn now to the reverse association—that is, between an *improvement* in environmental quality and the GNP. In the absence of policies to protect or improve the environment, a discussion of this relationship would parallel that above. Thus, no firm conclusion could be drawn without looking at changes in the composition of GNP, the composition of pollutants, and whether the improvement increased labor and capital productivity.

However, the issue is even more complicated if the reduction in pollution is partially or totally a result of environmental policies. The expenditures generated by these policies will have different effects on GNP, depending on who undertakes them and whether they are for investment goods or noninvestment goods and services such as labor, fuel, consumption items, or raw materials used in production.

For technical reasons (GNP includes final, not intermediate goods and labor), business expenditures for the operation and maintenance of pollution control equipment will tend to show up as a reduction in GNP. In effect, these expenditures divert labor and material away from items counted in the GNP and toward the production of a cleaner environment, which is not counted in the GNP. However,

---

1. A. Sudar, The Social and Economic Implications of Eutrophication in the Canadian Great Lakes Basin (January 1978) (unpublished report prepared for the Pollution from Land Use Activities Reference Group, Environment Canada).

similar operation and maintenance expenditures by consumers or by the government will show up as a change in the composition of GNP, but not necessarily in its level.

Expenditures to purchase pollution control equipment, whether by business, consumers, or the government, may not have any short-term effects on GNP. Indeed, GNP may increase slightly if these outlays serve to employ previously unemployed workers. Yet the longer term effects could be in the opposite direction. Some observers believe that for each 1 percent of capital diverted to the production of a cleaner environment from production of goods and services conventionally included in the GNP, ordinary GNP will eventually decline about one-third of 1 percent.[2] The fact that short-term and long-term effects may be in opposite directions explains why statements that "environmental regulation creates more jobs than it destroys" are compatible with seemingly contradictory statements that "environmental regulation dampens productivity and growth."

MODIFYING CONVENTIONALLY MEASURED GNP

There have been a number of efforts over the years to modify the conventional income and product accounts and the GNP in order to obtain either a better measure of production or of social well-being.[3] Those investigators explicitly interested in measures of well-being have recognized the problems discussed above and have suggested ways of more adequately accounting for the environment.

The best-known alternative measure of well-being is the measure of economic welfare (MEW) devised by Nordhaus and Tobin.[4] The MEW is largely a rearrangement of items of the national accounts. In addition, however, they have added imputations for items not covered in the conventional national accounts and the GNP: household work, leisure, and the services consumers derive from durable goods such as autos, boats, and appliances. Nordhaus and Tobin also include a correction (in the negative direction) for the "disamenities of urbanization." This correction is intended to include the unpleasantness of environmental pollution along with other characteristics of urban life

---

2. Labor diversion is even more serious under the same analysis. Presumably a 1 percent diversion of labor will lead to a 0.66 percent decline in output.

3. These efforts have been summarized in B. Campbell & J. Peskin, Expanding Economic Accounts and Measuring Economic Welfare: A Review of Proposals (Oct. 1979) (report prepared for the Measures of Economic Well-Being Branch, Environmental and Nonmarket Economics Division, Bureau of Economic Analysis, Department of Commerce, Washington, D.C.).

4. W. Nordhaus & J. Tobin, *Is Growth Obsolete?*, in ECONOMIC GROWTH (F. Thomas Juster ed. 1972).

that are disamenities to some: "litter, congestion, noise, insecurity, large buildings, and advertisements offensive to taste."

Since it is not possible to determine how much of Nordhaus and Tobin's correction is due to environmental deterioration alone, the MEW approach does not appear to be a satisfactory procedure for accounting for environmental changes. In addition, one could question the underlying premise behind the statistical procedure used to obtain the urban disamenity estimate: namely, that a higher urban income, relative to rural incomes, is necessary to compensate for urban disamenities. It is not difficult to imagine how urban incomes could be higher even if urban life were perceived to be superior to rural life. If, for example, urban living space were limited, and as a consequence, the supply of certain labor skills were also limited, higher urban incomes might simply reflect strong demand relative to limited supply of both labor and land.

In any event, the urban disamenity correction proposed by Nordhaus and Tobin appears to be fairly small. Of the total MEW of about $1200 billion that Nordhaus and Tobin estimate for 1965 (1958 dollars), the disamenity correction has a negative value of about $35 billion or 3 percent of the total. However, ordinary GNP in 1965 was about $618 billion (in 1958 dollars). Thus Nordhaus and Tobin's disamenity correction relative to GNP is more significant, about 6 percent of the total. Again, it should be remembered that the portion of this percentage due solely to environmental factors is unknown.

The Economic Council of Japan has attempted a more direct approach to account for the environment as part of their own measure of national well-being.[5] Like Nordhaus and Tobin, their net national welfare (NNW) measure is largely a rearrangement of national account items supplemented by imputations for the services of government capital, consumer durables, leisure, and other nonmarket activities. While there is a negative adjustment for urbanization, the environment is treated separately. First, there is a negative adjustment for "environmental maintenance costs." These are defined to equal the costs of operating and maintaining pollution control equipment plus the annualized capital costs of purchasing it. (This is analogous to the annual costs the Council on Environmental Quality reports each year in its *Annual Report.*) Second, there is a negative adjustment for remaining pollution not yet controlled. This adjustment is estimated by the approximate cost of reducing pollution to 1955 levels.

5. Economic Council of Japan, NNW Measurement Committee, *Measuring Net National Welfare of Japan* (April 30, 1974) (report prepared for the Japanese Ministry of Finance, Tokyo).

While there is a superficial appeal to subtracting both of these items from GNP to obtain a better welfare measure, the approach is deficient on two grounds. First, it confuses the costs of pollution control with the social gains from pollution control. In principle, the gains can be far greater or far less than the costs. Second, as the environment gets cleaner, the "environmental maintenance costs" will increase. This increase may be matched by a decrease in the estimate of the adjustment for remaining pollution since remaining pollution will be less. As a result, the Japanese NNW may increase, show no change, or even decrease when environmental quality improves. This makes it an unsatisfactory modification to the GNP accounts.

In contrast to the Nordhaus–Tobin MEW, the environmental adjustment of the Japanese NNW is fairly substantial. For 1965 it was about 12 percent of their GNP. Interestingly, the Japanese have a separate correction for urban disamenities. In contrast to the MEW, the urban disamenities are confined to time costs of commuting and the cost of traffic accidents. Nevertheless, the value of this negative correction is about 3 percent of NNW—about equal to the percentage share of urban disamenity in the Nordhaus–Tobin MEW.

A FRAMEWORK FOR MODIFYING THE TRADITIONAL ACCOUNT STRUCTURE

Disappointment with the ability of the conventional accounts to measure environmental changes has led to some additional suggestions for modifying the aggregate measures. For example, Olson, among others, has suggested that GNP be reduced by an amount equal to the social damage from pollution.[6] This reduction, in principle, would equal the amount of consumption expenditures incurred to "defend" against the disamenities, plus an additional amount people would be willing to pay to eliminate any remaining disamenities.

Other adjustments are possible. Herfindahl and Kneese have suggested that GNP be reduced by an amount equal to pollution control expenditures in the belief that this would be a suitable proxy for the amount of social damage caused by the pollution.[7] It also could be argued that NNP should be reduced by an amount that reflects any deterioration in the stock of environmental capital. This concept of the environment as a stock of a depreciable capital that generates in-

---

6. M. Olson, *The Treatment of Externalities in National Income Statistics*, in PUBLIC ECONOMICS AND THE QUALITY OF LIFE 219 (L. Wingo & A. Evans eds. 1977).

7. O. Herfindahl & A. Kneese, *Measuring Social and Economic Change: Benefits and Costs of Environmental Pollution*, in THE MEASUREMENT OF ECONOMIC AND SOCIAL PERFORMANCE 441 (M. Moss ed. 1973).

come forms another basis for modifying the standard accounting system.

This framework is based on the view that the environment, like the capital embodied in ordinary plant and equipment, generates useful services.[8] Also, like ordinary capital, environmental capital is in finite supply, and, for this reason, has a "scarcity" value. Unlike ordinary capital, the services of environmental capital are not bought and sold in the marketplace. This lack of a market not only means that some market substitute must be found for allocating these services among those in society demanding them, it also means that the true "scarcity" value of these services cannot be readily observed.

Suppose for the moment that a price could be set for environmental capital services and that it would be possible to vary this price and observe the quantity of services demanded. In other words, a demand curve could be established for each user of the service. Let us further suppose that the environmental service in question is that provided by clean air and consider the demand for this service by business. Except to serve the needs of its employees, business does not demand clean air per se. Clean air, however, provides a readily available source of oxygen for combustion and a convenient place to dispose of the waste products associated with this combustion as well as certain wastes associated with other processing.

Some of these uses are, of course, more essential than others. The "oxygen" service of clean air is critical since the business could not function without it. The demand for this service is thus very high. The disposal service, on the other hand, is less crucial—economists would say more marginal—since other options for reducing the amount of wastes disposed to the air are available to the business. These include the installation of pollution control equipment and changes in the level and mix of products.

However, these other options are expensive either in terms of equipment costs or in forgone sales and profits. If a price were established for the use of clean air, the business would presumably pay this price as long as it were slightly less than the unit cost of the least costly alternative waste reduction option.

Thus, the air offers a valuable disposal service in addition to other valuable services. These are, in principle, just as important to the business as labor, capital, and material services. The modified accounting framework to be discussed below acknowledges explicitly this

---

8. For purposes of this paper, environmental capital will be defined to include the air and those portions of land and water which are not privately owned. Thus, the term "environment" refers to only the *physical* environment.

similarity between environmental capital services and the services of
other inputs that are purchased.

To clearly distinguish consumers from businesses, assume for the
moment that consumers do not demand the air for disposal purposes
—an assumption that eventually will be dropped. Assume they demand clean air for life support, good health, and aesthetics. As noted
above, some of the business demand for air—the demand for disposal
services—is marginal since alternatives for these services exist. It is
controversial to make a similar assumption that some portion of the
demand for clean air by consumers is marginal. Many persons believe
that clean air is a "right" and that the concept of a finite price for
clean air is beyond imagination. Yet it is essential to assume that consumers would be willing to pay a finite price for clean air if the damages from air pollution are to be measured. This assumption is necessary to implement our suggested accounting structure.

If the services of environmental capital are to be entered into a national accounting structure, two accounting entries will be required.
One will describe the productive services the environment provides to
business and other consumers of environmental services. This will be
entered on the left-hand side of the business accounts and the consolidated national account, along with the other productive inputs. A
second entry will describe any resulting loss of environmental services or damage to consumers resulting from the use of the environment by business and other sectors. Since this damage can be viewed
as a "bad" produced by the business (as opposed to a "good"), it will
be entered negatively on the right-hand side of the business accounts
and the consolidated national account, along with the other components of output. Since, in general, these two entries will not be equal,
a balancing entry will be required if accounting balance is to be maintained.

These entries are not presently captured in the accounts since the
services of the environment are not priced. However, policy changes
could alter the situation. For example, if effluent charges were imposed on business, the value of the environmental services to them
will be reflected in their ordinary accounting. If these charges cover
the full value of the services, no additional input entry would be required. Similarly, if polluters were required to compensate consumers
suffering environmental damage, and if these payments covered the
full extent of the damage, an additional output entry would also not
be required. Such policies involving pollution charges and compensation appeal to economists since they promote efficient allocation of
environmental resources. Another attractive feature is that they
would help correct the faulty treatment of the environment in the

current national accounts. However, the ensuing discussion will assume that such a "full coverage" effluent fee-compensation scheme does not exist.

A MODIFIED ACCOUNTING STRUCTURE[9]

The above framework suggests a procedure for modifying the conventional income and product accounts so that they can capture certain features of the environment that are presently ignored. New account aggregates can be defined that better reflect changes in the demand for environmental services and in environmental quality.

The accounts modified to reflect environmental services are rather similar to those in the conventional accounting structure. The consolidated GNP account is a combination of production accounts in four sectors: industries, governments, households, and the environment (nature). In order to make them more understandable to those familiar with the conventional accounts, conventional as well as new entries are used. There are no new entries for current pollution control outlays since these are already included in the conventional accounts. However, it is probably useful to identify these costs separately, as has been done by the Bureau of Economic Analysis (Department of Commerce) since 1972.

Industries

The typical industry account shown in Table 1 contains three new entries that ordinarily would be absent from a conventional account of the industry's inputs and outputs. Item 11 accounts for environmental services and item 16 accounts for damages.[10] Environmental services, because they are "free," are like a subsidy to the industry. Therefore, they are entered as a negative input. Item 12 is the arithmetic difference between items 16 and 11. It assures that the modified accounts balance. Since it is defined as the difference between the service benefit of the environment and the "disbenefit" of environmental damage, it is labeled "net" environmental benefit.[11] The

---

9. This section is based on H. Peskin & J. Peskin, *The Valuation of Nonmarket Activities in Income Accounting,* 24 REV. OF INCOME & WEALTH 71 (March 1978) and H. Peskin, *A National Accounting Framework for Environmental Assets,* 2 J. ENVT'L ECON. & MANAGEMENT 255 (1976).

10. These are all damages—not just to consumers, but to any agents in the economy that are damaged (including other businesses).

11. Net environmental benefit is shown as the difference between the environmental damages entry and the services entry. However, since damages and services are entered negatively, it actually is equal to the absolute value of the services less the absolute value of the damages.

TABLE 1

INDUSTRY PRODUCT ACCOUNT (TYPICAL SECTOR)

Input	Output
1. Purchases from other industrial sectors	13. Sales to private sector (current account) 　a. To other industries 　b. To households 　c. Exports
2. Compensation of employees and proprietors (incl. rental income)	
3. Profits with inventory valuation and capital consumption adjustment 　a. Profits tax 　b. Profits after tax 　c. Inventory valuation and capital consumption adjustment	14. Sales to government 15. Sales for gross investment
4. Net interest	
5. Imports	
6. Transfer payments	
7. Indirect taxes	
8. Subsidies received (−)	
9. Capital consumption allowances	
GROSS INDUSTRY SECTOR INPUT	GROSS INDUSTRY SECTOR OUTPUT
11. Environmental services (−) 　a. Air 　b. Water 　c. Land	16. Environmental damages (−) 　a. Air 　b. Water 　c. Land
12. Net environmental benefit (1.16−1.11)*	
MODIFIED GROSS INDUSTRY SECTOR INPUT	MODIFIED GROSS INDUSTRY SECTOR OUTPUT

*1.16, 1.11, etc., means item 16, item 11, etc., table 1.

modified industry account input and output totals equal the conventional input and output totals less the absolute value of environmental damage.

Governments

As we noted earlier, the conventional governmental product account is rather simple. Similarly, the modified account shown in Table 2 is very simple since it contains only those additional entries that ac-

TABLE 2

GOVERNMENTAL PRODUCT ACCOUNT

Input	Output
1. Purchases from industry (1.14)	7. Governmental goods and services
2. Compensation of employees	
3. Imports	
GOVERNMENTAL INPUT	GOVERNMENTAL OUTPUT

5. Environmental services (–)
   a. Air
   b. Water
   c. Land
	8. Environmental damages (–)

6. Net environmental benefit (2.8–2.5)	
MODIFIED GOVERNMENTAL INPUT	MODIFIED GOVERNMENTAL OUTPUT

count for the government's use of the environment, the resulting damage, and the necessary balancing entry.

Households

The conventional accounts assume very little household production takes place (primarily accounted for by nonprofit institutions and the services of domestics). The focus of conventional accounts on activities that reflect market transactions precludes consideration of the "outputs" from keeping up a house, preparing meals, raising children, and do-it-yourself projects.[12]

Households are far more important in our modified accounts. Primarily because of the automobile, households account for a substantial portion of environmental damage and associated use of the air for disposal services. Households also enjoy the services of the water and, as a result, contribute to water pollution, although to a much lesser extent than in the case of air pollution.[13]

Households are unique among the producing sectors since most of the environmental damage they cause (as a result of their consumption of environmental services) is inflicted within the household sec-

---

12. The one major nonmarket activity associated with households that is included in the accounts—the imputation for the implicit "rents" from owner-occupied housing—is included in the business sector.

13. Sewered households do not, in our system, pollute the environment. Sewered wastes are inputs to municipal treatment works, an industrial sector, which is credited with any resulting environmental damage.

tor itself. In contrast, industries and government tend to inflict damage outside their own sector. The modified household account is shown in Table 3.

TABLE 3
HOUSEHOLD PRODUCT ACCOUNT

Input	Output
1. Purchases of intermediate goods from industry (1.13.b)	9. Services to households a. Nonprofit institutions b. Domestics
2. Compensation of employees and proprietors	
3. Imports	
4. Surplus of nonprofit institutions	
5. Capital consumption allowances	
GROSS HOUSEHOLD INPUT	GROSS HOUSEHOLD OUTPUT
7. Environmental services (−) a. Air b. Water c. Land	10. Environmental damages (−) a. Air b. Water c. Land
8. Net environmental benefit (3.10−3.7)	
MODIFIED GROSS HOUSEHOLD INPUT	MODIFIED GROSS HOUSEHOLD OUTPUT

Nature

The modified accounting system differs most markedly from the conventional system in its inclusion of nature as a producing sector. (See Table 4.) Nature is shown to produce all environmental asset services and to "consume" environmental damages. Nature also must be included because it generates a substantial portion of environmental damage. For example, a large portion of dissolved solids in water have a natural origin and, on average, naturally generated particulates and nitrogen oxides (other than nitrogen dioxide) greatly exceed the manmade production of these air pollutants.[14]

Some persons may have a philosophical objection to the idea of nature as a "polluter," but the concept is required for practical

14. *See, e.g.,* U.S. ENVT'L PROTECTION AGENCY, AIR QUALITY CRITERIA FOR NITROGEN OXIDES 3-1 (1971) and MIDWEST RESEARCH INSTITUTE, 1 PARTICULATE POLLUTANT SYSTEMS STUDY at Tables 4.1-1 and 4.1-2 (1971).

TABLE 4

NATURAL PRODUCTION

Input	Output

1. Environmental damages (including those naturally generated)
   a. Air
   b. Water
   c. Land
	2. Environmental services
	
	 3. Net environmental effect

NATURAL SECTOR INPUT	NATURAL SECTOR OUTPUT

reasons. Available estimates of damages due to air and water pollutants cannot distinguish between damages from pollutants that have a human origin and damages from those with a natural origin. Rather than attribute all the damage to nonnatural causes, it is more accurate to prorate the total damage between the two sources.

Consolidated Gross Product Account

The above accounts can be consolidated into a modified gross product account, as in Table 5. Inspection of this account indicates that modified GNP equals conventional GNP minus environmental damage. Actually this relationship is an identity: it is necessarily true because of the way we chose to arrange the entries into our accounting structure. However, a number of other arrangements are possible, each leading to its own formula relating the conventional GNP to a "modified" GNP.

To show this, the following notations are defined:

VA = charges against conventional GNP
GNP = conventional GNP
GNP^i = modified GNP, definition i (i = 1, 2, 3, and 4)
ES = environmental services
NEB = net environmental benefit
ED = environmental damage

Since the left-hand side and the right-hand side of the consolidated accounts must balance, the following identity holds:

$$VA + NEB - ES = GNP - ED$$

As noted, this identity implies the following "definition" of modified GNP:

$$GNP^1 = GNP - ED \qquad \text{(Definition 1)}$$

TABLE 5

CONSOLIDATED NATIONAL INCOME AND PRODUCT ACCOUNT

Input	Output
1. Compensation of employees and proprietors (incl. rental income) (1.2 + 2.2 + 3.2)	14. Personal consumption (1.13.b + 3.9)
	15. Gross private domestic investment (1.15)
2. Profits with inventory valuation and capital consumption adjustment (1.3) a. Profits tax b. Profits after tax c. Inventory valuation and capital consumption adjustment	16. Exports (1.13.c)
	17. Imports (−) (1.5 + 2.3 + 3.3)
3. Net interest (1.4)	18. Governmental goods and services (2.7)
NATIONAL INCOME	
5. Transfer payments (1.6)	
6. Indirect taxes (1.7)	
7. Subsidies (−) (1.8)	
8. Statistical discrepancy	
NET NATIONAL PRODUCT	
10. Capital consumption (1.9 + 3.5)	
CHARGES AGAINST GROSS NATIONAL PRODUCT	GROSS NATIONAL PRODUCT
12. Environmental services (−) (1.11 + 2.5 + 3.7) a. Air b. Water c. Land	19. Environmental damages (−) (1.16 + 2.8 + 3.10 + 4.2) a. Air b. Water c. Land
13. Net environmental benefit (5.16–5.9)	
CHARGES AGAINST MODIFIED GROSS NATIONAL PRODUCT	MODIFIED GROSS NATIONAL PRODUCT

However, as noted, accounting arrangements are arbitrary and other arrangements are possible as long as the accounts balance. For example, by adding ED and ES to both sides and noting that $NEB = ES - ED$, a new identity can be formed.

$$VA + ES = GNP + ES$$

which leads to a new definition:

$$GNP^2 = GNP + ES \qquad \text{(Definition 2)}$$

Similarly, by adding only *ES* to both sides and again noting that $NEB = ES - ED$ we can find a third definition of modified GNP:

$$GNP^3 = GNP + NEB \qquad \text{(Definition 3)}$$

Finally, by first adding *ES* to both sides and then subtracting *NEB* from both sides, we can find a fourth definition:

$$GNP^4 = GNP \qquad \text{(Definition 4)}$$

Thus modified GNP can be defined alternatively as conventional GNP less damage, conventional GNP plus environmental services, conventional GNP plus net environmental benefit, or simply as equal to conventional GNP. These definitions are by no means equivalent, but they are all *consistent* with the above modified accounting structure. The pros and cons of these alternatives will be discussed in the next section.

Note first, however, that the modified form of the other conventional national account aggregates, net national product (NNP) and national income (NI), can be defined in terms of the modified GNP. For example, since NNP is defined as GNP less capital consumption allowances, modified NNP can be defined as modified GNP less capital consumption allowances. Of course, as suggested earlier, the capital consumption allowances themselves may be modified to take account of the deterioration in environmental capital.

RELATIONSHIP BETWEEN THE ENVIRONMENT AND THE MODIFIED ACCOUNTS

Relationships between the modified accounts and the environment will be discussed in terms of the modified GNP concepts. Since the fourth definition of modified GNP is exactly the same as conventional GNP, we need only discuss the first three. The relationship between the environment and conventional GNP has already been discussed in this paper.

First Adjustment: $GNP^1 = GNP - ED$

We argued above that the conventional account aggregates do not always respond to changes in environmental quality in a manner that would make these aggregates acceptable indicators of well-being. Gross national product tended to increase with environmental deterioration and efforts to improve the environment would often be reflected by reductions in GNP, particularly if these efforts were under-taken by reallocation of business current account inputs or through shifts in investment.

The above definition of modified GNP clearly seems to perform much better as an indicator of well-being. GNP^1 appears to move "correctly" with respect to changes in ordinary GNP and to changes in environmental quality. It is perhaps for this reason that Olson rec-ommended this modification of conventional GNP.[15] Yet this first definition covers only part of the environmental relationship. The second definition covers another part.

Second Adjustment: $GNP^2 = GNP + ES$

The theoretical analysis behind the suggested modified accounting framework demonstrated that there was a beneficial environmental service associated with any observed environmental damage. This ser-vice, being "unpriced" and apparently "free," does not show up di-rectly in conventional GNP.

The second definition accounts directly for this unpriced input. Its use as an index of well-being would have interesting and perhaps con-troversial implications. For example, the difference in income be-tween a nonindustrialized, "less developed" society located in a trop-ical climate that generates environmental services in the form of warmth and abundant, freely available food, and an industrialized society located in a cold climate requiring a highly sophisticated agri-culture may be far less if income is measured by GNP^2; rather than ordinary GNP. (The difference might also be less under the first defi-nition if the industrialized society were also the more polluted.)

However, GNP^2 is prone to possible double counting of environ-mental services consumed by business. While these services may not be accounted for directly, they may be reflected in profits, which are captured by ordinary GNP. For example, a business that can dispose of its wastes in the ocean has a distinct advantage over a competitor that must treat its wastes. The opportunity to use the ocean's dis-posal service may show up as an increased profit rate for the business. In this example it would be superfluous for the national accountant to add in an amount equaling the value of the ocean service.

One interesting aspect of GNP^2 concerns its behavior with respect to pollution control expenditures. As noted, conventional GNP either is unaltered or declines, depending on whether the expenditure is by business, on capital or on current account, and on whether pollution control capital outlays divert capital from more "productive" uses.

---

15. *See* M. Olson, *supra* note 6, at 245.

On the other hand, assuming full employment, GNP^2 will always decline as pollution control expenditures increase. According to the theory behind our framework, pollution control expenditures mean that marketed goods and services are being substituted for environmental services. Thus, since ES will decline, GNP^2 will also decline.

Some may feel that because of this result, along with the potential for double counting, GNP^2 is a less desirable indicator of well-being than GNP^1. However, its focus on the benefits of ES is a strong point in its favor.

Third Adjustment: $GNP^3 = GNP + NEB$

Because NEP = ES – ED, this definition of modified GNP appears to be a compromise between GNP^1 and GNP^2. As an indicator of well-being it appears to move in the "correct" direction: increases in ES and decreases in ED imply increases in GNP^3. However, there are some circumstances under which GNP^3 has difficulty in moving in *any* direction. In the absence of technological change, decreases in environmental damage by business, ED, must be invariably accompanied by decreases in environmental services to business, ES. Thus, under policies of pollution control, NEB may remain essentially unchanged. For this reason, GNP^3 may not be very effective as an indicator of well-being after all.

IMPLEMENTATION OF THE FRAMEWORK

Efforts to design and implement the modified accounting framework have been under way for several years under National Science Foundation sponsorship.[16] This section describes these efforts and presents some crude estimates for the years 1972 and 1978.

This research has had to rely primarily on secondary sources of data assembled largely to support policy needs. As a result, the only type of environmental service for which national estimates of value are available is the disposal service provided by the air and water. Damage estimates are consequently confined to that resulting from the air and water pollution associated with the use of these disposal services. Also, many services of the environment are not captured in the available data on ES. Aesthetic and recreational services are two examples, although damage to aesthetics and recreation caused by waste disposal are supposedly accounted for in the estimates of ED. In addition, not all disposal services are accounted for, nor are all the pos-

---

16. *See* H. Peskin, *Accounting for the Environment,* 2 SOC. INDICATORS RESEARCH 191 (Sept. 1975) for a description of the research.

sible damages that are related to disposal. For example, the data do not cover the possible carcinogenic effects that may result from the disposal of dangerous chemicals in air or water.

The estimates of environmental damage are drawn from a number of studies of national air and water pollution damage sponsored by the Environmental Protection Agency. These studies have been critically reviewed by Freeman and we will not comment on them here.[17] Suffice it to say that they are generally extrapolations of smaller scale studies of air or water pollution damage in particular locations. There is no assurance that these studies were consistent in their estimation techniques or even in the time period covered. More important, there is no assurance that they used estimation techniques that yield good approximations of the true value to affected parties of eliminating the pollution. Thus the damage estimates are very rough and perhaps either too high or too low by a factor of two or three.[18]

There have been no national studies on the value of environmental disposal services. However, a proxy value of these services to polluters can be obtained by determining the prospective costs these polluters would incur if they were denied access to the disposal service.[19] These prospective costs, in turn, can be estimated by the expected control costs of reducing discharges to a very low level. Unfortunately, actual estimates used often represent the costs of applying specific suggested technologies and application of such technologies may not be the least-cost approach for all firms.[20]

In addition, it is difficult to estimate what the costs would be for an entire industry to adopt a specific control technology. Since the costs have yet to be incurred, they must be based on a mixture of engineering considerations and the experience of firms that have adopted similar technologies in the past. For all these reasons, the cost estimates are only crude approximations to the true value of environmental services to polluters.

The 1972 ES values for water were developed from the cost data by Gianessi and Peskin.[21] The ES values for air come from EPA's *The*

---

17. A. Freeman, The Benefits of Air and Water Pollution Control: A Review and Synthesis of Recent Estimates (December 1979) (report prepared for the U.S. Council on Environmental Quality, Washington, D.C.).

18. This estimate is based on the ranges given by Freeman. *Id.* at xiii-xv.

19. Note that these costs are not the same as the costs actually experienced as a result of pollution abatement efforts. These costs are already captured in the conventional accounts although they have only recently been separately identified by the Bureau of Economic Analysis in their Pollution Abatement Expenditures series. *See* F. Segel & F. Dreiling, *Pollution Abatement and Control Expenditures, 1972-6*, 58 SURVEY OF CURRENT BUS. 12 (Feb. 1978).

20. The technologies are suggested as guidelines for permit writers.

21. L. Gianessi and H. Peskin, *The Distribution of the Costs of Federal Water Control Policy*, 56 LAND ECON. 83 (Feb. 1980).

Economics of Clean Air (1972)[22] and Gianessi, Peskin, and Wolff.[23] For 1978, the 1972 values were increased to allow for economic growth and decreased to allow for the reduction in environmental disposal services as a result of the implementation of the 1970 Clean Air Act and the 1972 Federal Water Pollution Control Act Amendments. The degree of implementation is estimated as above by taking the ratio of reported pollution abatement capital outlays to Resources for the Future's estimates of required capital outlays.

All the ES and ED estimates are in units of dollars per year. Therefore, all investment cost estimates have been converted to an equivalent annualized form.[24] The modified accounts with the estimates are shown in Tables 6 and 7. All estimates are in current dollars.

According to these data, the level of environmental services or damages is rather small compared with major components of GNP such as personal consumption or gross private domestic investment. While in current dollars ES and ED are about the same in 1972 and 1978, there is clearly a decline in the value of both variables in 1978 if the effects of inflation are taken into account.

One of the biggest differences between 1972 and 1978 is in the balance between the use of environmental disposal services by a particular sector and the damages caused by that sector. Thus, in 1972, industry generated about twice as much damage to the air as it received in services from the air. On the other hand, households received disposal services from the air three times larger than the damages they caused (mostly due to automobile pollution). There was a much closer balance between damages and services for both industries and households in 1978.

It is apparent that, by any of the alternative definitions, the differences between conventional GNP and modified GNP are relatively small. The fact that the adjustments due to inclusion of the environment are small is not without significance and does perhaps help put the "environmental problem" in perspective. However, it should be kept in mind that *ES* reflects only disposal services. It may have been very much larger if other environmental services—such as recreation and aesthetic services—were included. Further research and data development will be required before comprehensive estimates of these other services can be made.[25]

22. U.S. ENVT'L PROTECTION AGENCY, THE ECONOMICS OF CLEAN AIR: ANNUAL REPORT OF THE ADMINISTRATOR (1972).

23. L. Gianessi, H. Peskin, & E. Wolff, *The Distributional Effects of Uniform Air Pollution Policy in the United States,* 93 Q. J. ECON. 281 (May 1979).

24. This conversion was done using a capital recovery factor formula as described in E. GRANT & W. IRESON, PRINCIPLES OF ENGINEERING ECONOMY (1960).

25. Presently, the National Science Foundation is sponsoring a Resources for the Future research project along these lines.

TABLE 6

1972 CONSOLIDATED NATIONAL INCOME AND PRODUCT ACCOUNT
(billions of 1972 dollars)

Input		Output	
1. Compensation of employees and proprietors (incl. rental income)	812.8	14. Personal consumption	733.0
2. Profits with inventory valuation and capital consumption adjustment	92.0	15. Gross private domestic investment	188.3
a. Profits tax 41.5		16. Exports	72.7
b. Profits after tax 54.6		17. Imports (−)	75.9
c. Inventory valuation & capital consumption adjustment −4.1		18. Governmental goods and services	253.1
3. Net interest	47.0		
NATIONAL INCOME	951.8		
5. Transfer payments	4.7		
6. Indirect taxes	111.0		

7. Subsidies (−) 3.6

8. Statistical discrepancy 1.7

 NET NATIONAL PRODUCT 1065.6

10. Capital consumption 105.4

 CHARGES AGAINST GROSS NATIONAL PRODUCT 1171.0

 GROSS NATIONAL PRODUCT 1171.0

12. Environmental services (−) 45.9
  a. Air, To: 23.8
    1. Industry 8.4
    2. Households 12.9
    3. Governments 2.5
    4. National NA
  b. Water, To: 22.1
    1. Industry 21.4
    2. Households .6
    3. Government .1
    4. Natural NA
  c. Land NA

19. Environmental damages (−) 30.0
  a. Air, By: 21.9
    1. Industry 16.3
    2. Households 4.3
    3. Governments .2
    4. National 1.1
  b. Water 8.1
  c. Land NA

13. Net environmental benefit 15.9

 MODIFIED CHARGES AGAINST GROSS NATIONAL PRODUCT 1141.0

 MODIFIED GROSS NATIONAL PRODUCT 1141.0

TABLE 7

1978 CONSOLIDATED NATIONAL INCOME AND PRODUCT ACCOUNT
(billions of 1978 dollars)

Input			Output	
1. Compensation of employees and proprietors (incl. rental income)		1447.2	14. Personal consumption	1350.8
			15. Gross private domestic investment	351.5
2. Profits with inventory valuation and capital consumption adjustment		167.7	16. Exports	207.2
a. Profits tax	84.5		17. Imports (–)	217.5
b. Profits after tax	121.5		18. Governmental goods and services	435.6
c. Inventory valuation & capital consumption adjustment	–38.3			
3. Net interest		109.5		
NATIONAL INCOME		1724.3		
5. Transfer payments		9.2		
6. Indirect taxes		178.1		

7.	Subsidies (−)		4.2
8.	Statistical discrepancy		3.3
	NET NATIONAL PRODUCT		1910.7
10.	Capital consumption		216.9
	CHARGES AGAINST GROSS NATIONAL PRODUCT		2127.6
12.	Environmental services (−)		45.1
	a. Air, To:	20.1	
	1. Industry	7.1	
	2. Households	10.9	
	3. Governments	2.1	
	4. National	NA	
	b. Water, To:	25.0	
	1. Industry	24.4	
	2. Households	.5	
	3. Governments	.1	
	4. Natural	NA	
	c. Land	NA	
13.	Net environmental benefit		14.1
	MODIFIED CHARGES AGAINST GROSS NATIONAL PRODUCT		2096.6

	GROSS NATIONAL PRODUCT		2127.6
19.	Environmental damages (−)		31.0
	a. Air, By:	18.2	
	1. Industry	9.3	
	2. Households	6.9	
	3. Governments	.3	
	4. National	1.7	
	b. Water	12.8	
	c. Land	NA	
	MODIFIED GROSS NATIONAL PRODUCT		2096.6

Comparisons of the four modified GNP concepts are shown in Table 8. GNP^4, which is equivalent to unmodified GNP, increased about 19 percent between 1972 and 1978 (constant dollars). GNP^1, which is smaller than unmodified GNP because of the subtraction of *ED,* had a growth rate about two percentage points higher, reflecting the beneficial effects of 1970 and 1972 pollution control legislation. Both GNP^2 and GNP^3, which are slightly larger than ordinary GNP, grew at a somewhat lower rate, although these two might have grown more if a more comprehensive measure of environmental services were available.

These movements in the various GNP concepts reflect movements in *ES, ED,* and *NEB.* Net environmental benefit is positive in both years, indicating that the value of disposal services exceeded the damages caused by the disposal. However, there was a substantial decline in *NEB* by 1978 because the disposal service value of the environment declined more rapidly than damages. This pattern should continue for future years since the prospective costs per unit of reduced damage, which are used as proxies for the value of environmental disposal services, are likely to rise as damages are reduced.

TABLE 8

COMPARISON OF MODIFIED GNP CONCEPTS AND ASSOCIATED
ENVIRONMENTAL BENEFITS

	1972 (billions of current dollars)	1972 (billions of constant dollars)	1978 (billions of current dollars)	1978 (billions of constant dollars)	Change in 1972 to 1978 (billions of constant dollars)	% Change in 1972 to 1978
ES	45.9	45.9	45.1	27.1	−18.8	−41
ED	30.0	30.0	31.0	20.5	−9.5	−32
NEB	15.9	15.9	14.1	6.6	−9.3	−58
GNP^1	1141.0	1141.0	2096.6	1378.7	237.7	21
GNP^2	1216.9	1216.9	2172.7	1426.3	209.4	17
GNP^3	1186.9	1186.9	2141.7	1405.8	218.9	18
GNP^4	1171.0	1171.0	2127.6	1399.2	228.2	19

It would be incorrect to draw too many conclusions from these data in view of the crudeness of the *ES* and *ED* estimates. Clearly, there is a lot of room for improvement in these estimates. Methods for obtaining better measures of environmental damage and control costs can be found in the extensive literature on cost-benefit analysis.[26] While environmental benefits due to policy are not the same thing as environmental damages due to the absence of policy, the techniques for estimating benefits can be used to estimate damages. Since much of this literature is already available, methods of improving benefit and cost estimates will not be discussed here.

SHOULD GNP BE MODIFIED?

The above estimates of potential modifications to GNP are extremely rough, reflecting the difficulties of imputing values to environmental services and damages. The most obvious deficiency of this attempt to adjust GNP is the inability to take account of the full range of services provided by the environment. While some adjustments for air and water pollution damage and their control can be made, other environmental adjustments are impossible to make with current data. They might significantly affect GNP.

These facts alone, however, do not argue against efforts to modify the conventional national economic accounts along the lines suggested. Since the new account entries in no way destroy the existing accounting system, they could be either accepted or ignored, depending on how one felt about the worthiness of imperfect estimates. Nevertheless, even modest efforts to develop and improve such data will be expensive. Thus it is reasonable to ask whether the effort is worth it.

The answer to this question depends, not only on the actual and perceived value of the new information and new GNP concepts that may emerge from the effort, but also on the perceived value of the current GNP and national accounting efforts. The reason for this latter dependence is that the new effort may divert scarce resources that go into the conventional accounts. It may also divert some of the attention the conventional accounts and, especially, GNP receives in the popular press.

Of course, those dissatisfied with the conventional GNP may welcome such diversions. But in all fairness, it must be recognized that the existing system serves important analytical and policy purposes. The national accounts, after all, have provided the basic data and indexes for describing economic activity and developing economic policy for nearly 50 years. Defenders of the existing national economic

---

26. *See, e.g.,* H. PESKIN & E. SESKIN, COST-BENEFIT ANALYSIS AND WATER POLLUTION POLICY (1975) and A. Freeman, *supra* note 17.

These references contain extensive bibliographies on the application of cost-benefit analysis to environmental problems.

accounts do not base their arguments on a mistaken belief that the GNP measures well-being, but rather on the position that any modifications may impair its analytical and policy usefulness. While they may see a need for better information on environmental and other factors that affect well-being, they argue that such data can be and should be collected independently of the national accounting system.[27]

There are two principal objections to this line of argument. In the first place, it assumes that the national accounts are adequate for economic analysis and policy. While the accounts may be adequate for traditional economic concerns—production, employment, inflation—that are reflected in the marketplace, in recent years there have been new economic concerns—the allocation of time in the household, development of human capital, management of environmental resources—that are only imperfectly reflected in the marketplace. Those who think these issues are important are not likely to find it of overriding importance to maintain the integrity of the existing accounting system.

The other objection is that any effort to develop independent data sets on items ignored by the conventional accounts is likely to be chronically underfunded and generally ignored as long as the conventional GNP and the national accounting activities maintain an official and singular status in the federal bureaucracy. Given this status, it is not surprising that the public places more importance on the GNP as a measure of well-being than do the experts.

Moreover, there are close interdependencies between market and nonmarket activities. Use of the environment, for example, is affected by a host of economic decisions by producers and consumers: the entrepreneur's choice of a production process, the consumer's decision to watch television or go fishing. An expanded national accounting system, rather than a set of independent data series, would reveal and permit easier analysis of these interdependencies. Also (and this is especially true for environmental data), much of the data in the conventional accounts and the additional data needed to expand the accounts and develop new GNP measures come from the same basic sources (e.g., the Census of Manufacturers) as the data now collected.

None of these arguments can be dismissed out of hand. While it does appear worthwhile to explore new methods of expanding the conventional GNP concepts, and while, for reasons of public visibility and efficient data collection, such efforts are probably best coordi-

---

27. *See, e.g.,* E. Denison, *Explanation of Declining Productivity Growth,* 59 SURVEY OF CURRENT BUS. 1 (Aug. 1979).

nated by the same federal bureaucracies that are responsible for the conventional accounts,[28] it would be unfortunate if they led to a weakening of the present national accounting method.

Any attempt to construct a better GNP will require new sources of funds. Costs can be kept down through the use of data already collected by various federal agencies, usually for their own administrative purposes. For example, estimates of environmental disposal services can be drawn from data currently being assembled as part of the rulemaking procedures of the Environmental Protection Agency. Also buried in various environmental impact statements is material that could be used to develop information on environmental damage.

With good planning and coordination, it should be possible to modify slightly the form by which data are collected and stored by the various administrative agencies so that they can more easily be incorporated into an expanded national accounting structure. It may be worthwhile for the heads of such agencies as the Environmental Protection Agency, the departments of Interior, Commerce, and Agriculture, and the Council on Environmental Quality to convene a committee for this purpose. It would be unfortunate if efforts to find better GNP measures were thwarted by a false belief that the costs of the effort are "too high"—a perception that overlooks the benefits of good interagency cooperation.

---

28. For this reason, it is unfortunate that the Bureau of Economic Analysis, the agency responsible for the national accounts, is terminating its recently established programs to conduct research on accounting for nonmarket activities.

Stationary Source Pollution Policy
and Choices for Reform
WINSTON HARRINGTON and ALAN J. KRUPNICK*

In response to the alleged adverse effects of regulation, the reconsideration of environmental policies now under way gives far more prominence to the economic implications of regulatory policies than has been the case in the past. Adverse economic effects associated with regulation, however, do not necessarily justify the abandonment of environmental policy objectives. Rather, these effects may be seen as emphasizing the importance of seeking alternative approaches.

The environmental policies with the greatest impact on the national economy are probably those that limit industrial air and water pollution. These policies are now under attack for imposing excessive compliance costs on households, firms, and government and for retarding innovation and investment. These costs have, in turn, been linked to excessive reliance on technology-based standards and to cumbersome and erratic procedures for obtaining permits for construction of new plant and equipment.

In this paper we briefly discuss the approach to stationary source air and water pollution that was formulated in the early 1970s and point out some of its limitations. We next examine some major modifications to this approach put in place in 1977 and discuss in detail the merits of a number of recent substantive and procedural reforms and their effects on the economy. Some of these reforms involve greater use of economic incentives in pollution abatement policy.

TECHNOLOGY-BASED STANDARDS

Congress enacted the Clean Air Act Amendments (CAA) in 1970 and the Federal Water Pollution Control Act Amendments (FWPCA) in 1972. Although earlier environmental pollution statutes were on the books,[1] these two acts represented a fundamental change in the degree and kind of federal intervention to protect environmental quality.[2]

---

*Winston Harrington and Alan J. Krupnick are fellows in the Quality of the Environment Division, Resources for the Future.

1. For a discussion of federal pollution legislation prior to 1970, see A. KNEESE & C. SCHULTZE, POLLUTION, PRICES, AND PUBLIC POLICY 39-50 (1975).

2. *Id.* at 51. *See also* A. Freeman, *Air and Water Pollution Policy,* in CURRENT ISSUES IN U.S. ENVIRONMENTAL POLICY 12 (P. Portney ed. 1978).

The most important innovation in these two statutes was their extensive reliance on technology-based emission standards for waste dischargers. In the technology-based approach, the abatement regulations for an industrial category are determined solely by considering the abatement technologies available and are applied uniformly to all plants in the category.

The FWPCA required EPA to establish effluent limitations specifying, for each industrial category, the pollution abatement achievable by the best practicable technology currently available (BPT) and the best available technology economically achievable (BAT).[3] Industrial dischargers were required to meet the BPT and BAT standards by 1977 and 1983, respectively, but were not required to adopt the technologies suggested by EPA as guidelines. The actual discharge limitation applicable to a particular plant was specified in an effluent discharge permit. In most states, the writing of permits has been delegated to the state water quality agency.[4]

The Clean Air Act Amendments of 1970 required EPA to designate "criteria pollutants" and to establish national ambient air quality standards sufficient to protect the public health and welfare.[5] Each state was then required to prepare and implement a state implementation plan which would achieve the ambient standards. This provision did not require the states to base their standards on particular technologies, but most states followed this course. In addition, EPA was directed by Congress to issue new source performance standards by industrial category for newly constructed plants. These standards were supposed to reflect the best performance in commercial operation at the time of promulgation, and were to be revised every few years.[6] Unlike the Federal Water Pollution Control Act, the Clean Air Act did not require sources to have permits. However, every state implementation plan required new sources or modifications of existing sources to obtain construction permits, and in addition many required all sources to obtain periodically renewable operating permits.

---

3. *See* 33 U.S.C. § 1311(b)(1)(A) (1976) for BPT timetable. For BAT timetable, *see id.* § 1311(b)(2)(A) (Supp. II 1978).

4. One apparent exception to the technology-based standards occurred in so-called "water quality limited" streams. If it was estimated that application of BPT and BAT would not achieve the water quality objectives for a particular watershed, then permit writers were able to require dischargers to meet more stringent standards. 33 U.S.C. § 1312(a) (1976). Nonetheless, the emphasis remained on what technology could do, rather than on finding the cost-effective method of achieving the water quality objectives.

5. Clean Air Act Amendments of 1970, §§ 108-109, Pub. L. No. 91-604, 81 Stat. 1678 (codified at 42 U.S.C. §§ 7408-7409 (Supp. II 1978)). Currently the criteria pollutants are carbon monoxide, nitrogen dioxide, sulfur oxides, ozone, hydrocarbons, particulates, and lead.

6. *Id.* § 111 (codified at 42 U.S.C. § 7411 (Supp. II 1978)).

THE 1977 ADJUSTMENT

Progress was made in improving air and water quality between 1972 and 1977, but the objectives of neither act were met.[7] In water policy this was neither surprising nor especially disturbing, because the interim goal of making the water safe for contact recreation was not supposed to be achieved until 1983. (In addition, the "fishable, swimmable" goal of the water act did not have the same legal force as the ambient air quality standards.) Perhaps for this reason, the 1977 Clean Water Act involved relatively minor changes to the 1972 statute. The most important of these changes was a reorientation of best available technology toward toxic pollutants. Under the 1977 amendments, EPA is required to establish BAT standards for 65 designated toxic and "other nonconventional" pollutants for each industrial category.[8] For biochemical oxygen demand (BOD), suspended solids, and pH—the so-called "conventional pollutants"—the old best available technology requirement was replaced by a requirement to meet best conventional technology (BCT) standards,[9] which were intended to be somewhat more stringent than the original best practical technology standards, but less stringent than BAT. The deadline for meeting the new BCT standards was postponed one year to July 1, 1984, while BAT standards for toxic pollutants were to be met within three years after promulgation, but in no case later than July 1, 1987.[10]

The primary ambient air quality standards were supposed to have been achieved by 1977, but that year came and went with many areas of the country—including most major metropolitan areas—having failed to achieve the standards for at least one criteria pollutant. In addition, in areas with air quality better than the standards, maintenance of air quality was not assured. Accordingly, the 1977 Clean Air Amendments made important changes to the Clean Air Act to address these problems of "nonattainment" and "prevention of significant deterioration" (PSD).[11]

---

7. "[D]ata from approximately 59 of the most polluted counties across the country show that violations of ambient air quality standards generally either stayed constant or decreased between 1974 and 1977." COUNCIL ON ENVIRONMENTAL QUALITY, TENTH ANNUAL REPORT 17 (1979). "The available evidence . . . suggests that water quality in the United States, while not showing vast improvement since the early 1970s is at least not getting any worse." *Id.* at 75.

8. 33 U.S.C. § 1317(a)(1) (Supp. II 1978).

9. *Id.* § 1311(b)(2)(E) (Supp. II 1978).

10. *Id.* § 1311(b)(2)(F) (Supp. II 1978).

11. 42 U.S.C. §§ 7470-7491 (Supp. II 1978). EPA had already promulgated rules covering nonattainment (41 Fed. Reg. 55,524 (1976)) and PSD (39 Fed. Reg. 42,510 (1974)). In the 1977 amendments these policies were given congressional sanction and made considerably more stringent and exacting. For a discussion of the differences between the EPA

Additional changes included the creation of a noncompliance penalty, which was to be imposed on any source not yet in compliance with applicable federal or state (SIP) regulations.[12] The economic incentive for firms to delay compliance was to be eliminated by setting the penalty equal to their cost savings from noncompliance.[13] Another section of the amendments redefined NSPS to include a "percent reduction" requirement.[14] The impetus for this change was the new source performance standards promulgated for coal-fired utility boilers which, under the 1970 Act, could be achieved by use of low-sulfur coal without installation of sulfur dioxide control equipment. By foreclosing such nontechnological responses to new source performance standards, the bias toward technology-based standards was strengthened.

ECONOMIC IMPLICATIONS OF CURRENT AIR AND WATER POLLUTION POLICY

As noted, 1977 brought changes intended to increase the effectiveness of the Clean Water and Clean Air acts, especially the latter. The realization is emerging, however, that these changes may be very costly. That possibility gives added impetus to the current discussion of environmental policy reform. Before discussing reform, we comment briefly on the economic disadvantages of the existing approach.

One of the principal criteria for judging air and water pollution policy is cost-effectiveness: the ability to achieve given environmental quality goals for the lowest possible cost.[15] For two reasons, technology-based standards do not perform well according to this criterion. First, because such standards are uniform within industrial categories, they cannot allow for the fact that the same pollutant discharged in different locations can have vastly different environmental effects. Second, such standards do not take adequate account of the large differences in abatement costs among dischargers even within the same industrial category.

Consideration of costs in establishing the various standards required by the Clean Air and Clean Water acts has almost always been

---

policies and the 1977 amendments, see J. Quarles, *Federal Regulation of New Industrial Plants,* 10 ENVT'L RPTR. (BNA) (Monograph No. 28: May 4, 1979).

12. 42 U.S.C. § 7420(a)(2)(A) (Supp. II 1978).

13. It was not until July 28, 1980 that final regulations were issued. *See* 45 Fed. Reg. 50,086 (1980) (to be codified in 40 C.F.R. § 66-67 (1981)).

14. 42 U.S.C. § 7411(f)(1) (Supp. II 1978).

15. Cost-effectiveness is related, but not identical, to economic efficiency. To judge the efficiency of a policy, we must estimate the benefits attributable to the policy and compare them to the costs. An efficient policy is cost-effective but not vice versa.

limited to an assessment of economic impact within an industry category, i.e., whether the standards would result in plant closings or unemployment. However, results based on such impacts are imperfectly related to cost-effectiveness: if standards must be uniform within industrial categories, the most cost-effective approach is probably to equate marginal abatement costs across industries.[16] It is apparent that EPA did not make cross-industry cost comparisons. Rough estimates of the marginal abatement costs of a sample of the best practicable technology standards promulgated under the Federal Water Pollution Control Act showed variation by a factor of 30.[17]

Although data do not exist to estimate the potential cost savings available nationally from increased cost-effectiveness, some studies suggest potential regional savings of over 80 percent.[18] Thus the cost savings may be significant given the fact that in the coming decade (1979–88) the average pollution abatement expenditures by manufacturing and utilities are expected to be $25 billion per year.[19]

Naturally, a policy which perfectly reflects the costs and benefits of abatement at thousands of sources is an unattainable ideal, but these estimates suggest that great improvements are possible, and help explain the intense current interest in alternative approaches.

Indirect Effects

Although the direct costs of environmental regulations are significant, some analysts think that the indirect effects on the overall economy are much more important. For one thing, the rigidities of the technology-based approach may inhibit technological innovation in this area, although this proposition is difficult to verify empiri-

---

16. However, if industries with high marginal abatement costs just happen to be located where the marginal damages are high, it may be more cost-effective to set standards with different marginal abatement costs in different industries.

17. The marginal abatement cost estimates varied from 10¢/kg of BOD removed for the large chicken-processing plant subcategory to $3.15/kg BOD for the small duck-processing plant subcategory. *See* A. Krupnick & W. Harrington, Equity and Efficiency in the Promulgation of Federal Regulation: The Case of EPA's Effluent Discharge Standards (Sept. 6, 1980) (paper presented at Allied Social Sciences Association Annual Meeting).

18. *E.g.*, U.S. ENVT'L PROTECTION AGENCY, AN ANALYSIS OF MARKET INCENTIVES TO CONTROL STATIONARY SOURCE NO_x EMISSIONS (Draft Oct. 1980).

19. COUNCIL ON ENVIRONMENTAL QUALITY, ELEVENTH ANNUAL REPORT (1980). A study prepared at Resources for the Future estimates expenditures due to implementation of the 1970 Clean Air and the Federal Water Pollution Control acts to be about $34 billion per year in manufacturing and utilities. Total national expenditures are expected to be $77 billion per year (1978$). *See* H. Peskin, Environmental Gains and Economic Losses: A Connection? (April 1980) (report prepared for the Environmental Assessment Council of the Academy of Natural Sciences, Philadelphia, Pa.).

cally.[20] Technology-based standards by no means eliminate the incentives for innovation. Because such standards are usually based on the "best" technology available (variously defined), they may promote the diffusion of existing technology. In addition, with a technology-based effluent standard, there is an incentive to introduce innovations which reduce the cost of meeting the standard so long as there is some assurance the standard will not be tightened in response.

Nonetheless, it seems clear that technology-based standards provide little incentive for innovations that reduce emissions below state-of-the-art. In fact, these standards may discourage such innovations if EPA always responds to them by making the standard more stringent. This response leads to the so-called "ratchet effect,"[21] which can affect incentives for abatement innovation at both new and existing plants. New plants are affected because EPA is supposed to revise new source performance standards to reflect "best available" technology. Existing plants are affected because their permits are of limited duration. If an existing plant adopts innovative technology that reduces pollutant discharges below the current discharge standard, it may find itself subject to a more stringent standard based on the new technology when the permit is renewed. When standards are ratcheted, only firms in the business of supplying abatement technology have incentives to develop pollution-reducing innovations. Because such firms typically supply end-of-pipe equipment only, opportunities for fundamental process innovations that reduce emissions may be lost.

Technology-based standards provide barriers to other types of innovation as well. Both the Clean Air and the Clean Water acts require new plants to meet more stringent emission limitations than existing plants through the use of new source performance standards.[22] This discrepancy between old and new plant requirements tends to reduce investment in plant and equipment, and remaining investment is diverted away from new plant construction and toward rehabilitation of older equipment. Innovation is retarded because much of it would be embodied in new plant investment. The tendency to "grandfather"

---

20. *See, e.g.,* A. Freeman, *Air and Water Pollution Policy,* in CURRENT ISSUES IN U.S. ENVIRONMENTAL POLICY 12, 56-57 (1978). If the technology-based standard requires a particular technology, there is no incentive at all for innovation. As noted, the air and water discharge standards we are discussing required performance equivalent to a designated technology. Nonetheless, firms appear to behave as if the designated technologies are required, an approach that minimizes their exposure to risk. *Id.*

21. R. Repetto, The Influence of Standards, Effluent Charges, and Other Regulatory Approaches on Innovation in Abatement Technology (Sept. 1980) (working paper for Center for Population Studies, Harvard University).

22. 42 U.S.C. § 7411 (Supp. II 1978) and 33 U.S.C. § 1316 (1976), respectively.

existing plants also works indirectly to inhibit innovation (and competition) by restricting entry.

Perhaps an even more serious consequence of the current approach is that it makes for a more uncertain business climate.[23] Plant managers contemplating investment in new plants face uncertainty about what future regulations will require and when the requirements will take effect. Moreover, the extensive permitting requirements have greatly increased the lead time required for construction of new facilities.[24] These uncertainties can substantially affect the profitability of new investment.

The "prevention of significant deterioration" (PSD) and nonattainment policies exacerbate the uncertainty problem. A new plant (or an expansion of an existing plant) to be built in either a PSD or a nonattainment area is subject to significant new regulatory requirements that may be extremely difficult to overcome. Inasmuch as investment in new plants is a primary source of economic growth, the importance of these policies is obvious.

Under the PSD policy, the "clean air" areas of the country have been subdivided into three classes.[25] In each class, a certain degradation of existing ambient air quality is permitted. These increments are approximately 2 percent of the primary national ambient standards in Class I areas, 25 percent in Class II, and 50 percent in Class III.[26]

In order to ensure that the increments are not violated, PSD requires a preconstruction review of proposed new or expanded industrial facilities. In this review the following are required at a minimum:

(a) monitoring of preconstruction air quality, if not previously done;

(b) demonstration, using air quality models, that construction of the plant will not violate any allowable increment, either around the plant or in any other region (this could be very important for plants located in Class II or III areas but which are upwind of Class I areas);

---

23. *See* A. Greenspan, *Investment Risk: The New Dimension of Policy,* 264 THE ECONOMIST 31 (Aug. 6, 1977).

24. Anecdotal evidence for the effect of environmental regulation on delay abounds. See, for example, the case studies found in CONGRESSIONAL RESEARCH SERVICE, LIBRARY OF CONGRESS, ENERGY DEVELOPMENT PROJECT DELAYS: SIX CASE STUDIES (Serial No. 96-7: 1979). However, we have been unable to find any systematic studies of the effects of regulation on construction delays.

25. *See* 42 U.S.C. § 7472 and § 7474 (Supp. II 1978).

26. Most national parks and wilderness areas were permanently designated Class I. All other areas were initially designated Class II. States are authorized to redesignate areas to Class I or III, but only after preparing an impact analysis and holding a public hearing. Class III designations also require legislative approval of local governmental units representing a majority of area residents. 42 U.S.C. § 7474(b) (Supp. II 1978).

(c) agreement to install best available control technology (BACT);
(d) commitment to conduct postconstruction monitoring; and
(e) a public hearing.

If all requirements are satisfied, EPA will issue a permit and the source may commence construction.[27]

With the possible exception of (d), each of these requirements is a potentially serious impediment to new plant construction. If previous air quality monitoring has not been adequate, it may take two years to establish a baseline. The need to demonstrate that increments will not be violated is potentially an even greater source of delay and uncertainty. Since air quality modeling is notoriously inexact, the stage is set for possibly lengthy litigation between opposing groups using competing models. The confusion will be exacerbated by the fact that the applicant will have to model not only his own plant but the proposed plants of others.

The requirement for best available control technology will be defined case-by-case for each applicant, though the adopted technology must be more effective than the applicable new source performance standards. This requirement may add considerably to the cost of abatement. Negotiation over the best available control technology could also be a significant source of delay and uncertainty.

The effect of the public hearing requirement on uncertainty and delay is unknown. It can be either an occasion for the establishment of communication between the company and the community in which it seeks to reside, or a tactical opportunity for interest groups opposed to construction for reasons that have little to do with air quality.

In "dirty air" areas, new or expanded plants are subject to the nonattainment policy,[28] the requirements of which are likely to be even more onerous than those of preventing significant deterioration. In the first place, the 1977 amendments to the Clean Air Act required the states to submit by July 1, 1979 revised state implementation plans to assure compliance with ambient air quality standards by the end of 1982 (with a possible extension of the deadline to 1987 for photochemical oxidants and carbon monoxide).[29] The new state implementation plans must put into effect a permit program for construction and operation of major new or modified sources (previously this was optional). Moreover, to obtain a permit, a firm wishing to install the new source must meet the following conditions:

---

27. To avoid confusion we use "source" to mean a discharge point. Thus, a plant can have several sources just as a firm can have several plants. In EPA usage "source" can refer to any of these entities.

28. 42 U.S.C. § 7502 (Supp. II 1978).

29. *Id.* § 7502(a) (Supp. II 1978).

(a) For those pollutants not meeting ambient standards, the plant must ensure that the total quantity of emissions does not increase.[30] This will probably mean that pollution reductions, or "offsets," greater than the source is expected to generate must be obtained from other sources of those pollutants. Alternatively, the states could force cleanup of existing sources in order to allow a sufficient margin for growth.

(b) The plant must install equipment that achieves a "lowest achievable emission rate" (LAER).[31] Like best available control technology, it is set on a case-by-case basis and is supposed to be more stringent than new source performance standards.

(c) The firm must demonstrate that its other plants within the state are in compliance.[32]

In addition, the state must show that it is making reasonable progress toward achieving the 1982 (or 1987) objectives of the state implementation plan.

In principle, the offset approach can be an effective and efficient way to achieve air quality objectives, although practical difficulties may arise if few dischargers of the relevant pollutants can be found.[33] However, this desirable feature may be overwhelmed by the other requirements of the nonattainment policy, which create special barriers for expansion of existing plants or construction of new ones. Probably the greatest source of uncertainty is the requirement that the state be making reasonable progress toward attainment.[34] Because fulfillment of this requirement is vitally affected by the behavior of air quality agencies within the state and by other firms, it is something over which the applicant has little or no control.

The prevention of significant deterioration and nonattainment provisions together were intended to make the national air quality program comprehensive—to bring the heavily polluted areas of the country up to some minimum standard, while protecting the quality of the air where it is still clean. Instead, these changes created the potential for a regulatory quagmire. Because air quality in every location must either be better or worse than national standards, one of these two policies will presumably apply everywhere. Moreover, because air quality in an area can be better than the ambient standard for one pollutant and worse for another, it is possible, even probable, that an area will be subject to *both* the prevention of significant deterioration and nonattainment policies. This is not unlikely since

---

30. *Id.* § 7503(1)(B) (Supp. II 1978).
31. *Id.* § 7503(2) (Supp. II 1978).
32. *Id.* § 7503(3) (Supp. II 1978).
33. *See* discussion regarding offsets, *infra.*
34. 42 U.S.C. § 7502(b)(3) (Supp. II 1978).

much of the country violates the oxidant standard while complying with the sulfur oxide standard. Overlap can also occur if emissions from a source located in a nonattainment area can cross into a Class I area. In either case, the source will be subject not only to separate requirements but even to two different air quality bureaucracies: EPA (for prevention of significant deterioration) and the local or state agency (for nonattainment).

In sum, the existing structure of air and water pollution regulation, particularly the prevention of significant deterioration and nonattainment provisions of the Clean Air Act, is a potentially serious obstacle to economic growth in the United States. The direct resource costs of these policies may not be the main problem. Indeed, while the econometric studies discussed elsewhere in this volume[35] do not ascribe much of our current poor economic performance to environmental regulation, these models are driven only by reported or estimated direct expenditures on environmental protection. Regulatory delay and uncertainty may be causing economic distress that these models attribute to other causes or to the "unexplained residual." Any discussion of reform, therefore, must consider both the expenditures necessitated by regulation and their effects on uncertainty.

PROCEDURAL REFORMS

One general approach to regulatory reform is to alter the procedures used to develop and implement environmental regulations. Such changes can reduce both direct expenditures and the losses associated with regulatory delay and uncertainty. Several of these proposed procedural reforms—in particular, in rulemaking and permit procedures, delayed compliance for innovations, cost-effectiveness standards, and improved federal-state coordination—may have clear macroeconomic impacts.

Rulemaking Reforms

Of the myriad proposals advanced to reform the process of setting technology-based standards, we discuss reforms of the information-gathering phase of writing effluent limitations, the use of subcategorization, and the timeliness of promulgating regulations.

Improving Information Flow

Writing any technology-based standard requires gathering and organizing information on waste treatment practices, costs, and efflu-

---

35. See the papers by Haveman and Portney in this volume.

ents from industry sources, control equipment vendors, and industry experts. Typically, outside consultants, acting more or less in close consultation with an EPA project officer, are hired to produce a "development document" or "background information" report containing this information. This process came under attack during the BPT rulemaking because contractors, rather than EPA, initially recommended effluent limitations. Contracts were often let to the lowest bidder regardless of credentials, and qualified contractors were accused of underbidding on initial work in order to obtain future, sole source contracts. Finally, the range of technological alternatives considered by the contractors was too narrow.

The practice of having contractors recommend limitations has been modified for establishment of the BAT standards in response to questions about EPA's lack of oversight over the information flow.[36] But, pressures of time, funding, and custom will still limit the range of technological alternatives considered by the contractor for best available technology. Because many firms may be unwilling to incur the higher risk of enforcement action associated with a compliance strategy that departs from the suggested technology, restrictions on the options considered may impose compliance costs that are higher than necessary. Moreover, this problem is exacerbated for BAT because the range of pollutants, and therefore abatement options, is so much greater than for best practicable technology.

One approach might be for EPA to fund simultaneously a number of competitive development documents, with EPA acting as arbiter and synthesizer. Doing so would ensure that information from many points of view would be brought into the process at a sufficiently early stage to affect the outcome.[37] Doubtless this approach would substantially increase the cost of preparing a development document because not one but two or three draft documents would be prepared. It would also mean more work for EPA: the agency would no longer be able to issue the contractor's draft report as the development document without substantial changes, as it often did in earlier rulemaking procedures. In the long run, however, the use of competitive development documents might significantly reduce the administrative cost and thereby the total social cost of a regulation. The use of information from wider points of view may make the industry

---

36. Personal communication with Robert Dellinger, Project Officer, Effluent Guidelines Division, U.S. Environmental Protection Agency, Washington, D.C. (Dec. 12, 1980).

37. While information from a wide range of sources does make it into the process, most of it enters after the regulation has been proposed. By this time the broad outlines of the regulation usually have been set, and the regulation can be changed only slightly.

more receptive to the regulation, reducing the chance of a court challenge, and thereby reducing administrative cost.

Greater Attention to Subcategorization

The Environmental Protection Agency issues separate regulations for groups of firms in an industry with similar air or water problems. This "subcategorization" of industry is required to tailor suggested technologies and effluent limitations to specific processes, products, or other industry characteristics. It is also used for equity reasons, to cushion the impacts on industry segments, which otherwise would be especially hard hit by the regulation. This practice plays a central role in water pollution rulemaking and a more indirect role in the state implementation planning process for air pollution control. Subcategorization can affect not only control costs for firms placed in one category or another but also the competitiveness of the industry. Where subcategorization is used primarily to give smaller or older plants more lenient treatment, competition is enhanced since exit from the industry may be prevented. Competitive industries may be less resistant to downward pressures on prices and wages, which in turn may make anti-inflation policy more effective. Also, more subcategories for smaller, older plants may promote efficiency if the marginal compliance costs for these plants are higher than for larger, newer plants at a given treatment level. However, greater subcategorization has its drawbacks. Reducing the likelihood of exit by favoring smaller or older plants interferes with the turnover of capital stock in the industry and thereby reduces productivity. These effects are especially pronounced when existing plants are favored over new plants, as is currently the case.

Because of the mixed effects of subcategorization, no simple policy option emerges. Nonetheless, explicit attention should be given to the incentives offered to firms in the industry instead of concentrating solely on questions of equity or technology.

It should not be too surprising that greater subcategorization could emerge as a reform. Effluent fees, marketable permits, and other traditional economic incentive policies allow environmental targets to be reached at minimum resource cost. At the limit, if government established subcategories so as to equalize marginal treatment costs (a subcategory for nearly every firm might be needed), this optimal resource allocation could be approximated. Yet, it is difficult to imagine how such a system would work in practice. For instance, small plants do not necessarily have higher marginal costs of compliance, while an old plant may not necessarily have all old equipment. And, informational demands would probably be prohibitive.

Permit Reform

Permits are used extensively in both air and water pollution policy to promote compliance with regulations. Some options which could reduce uncertainty and delay follow.

Extend Permit Life

Increasing the life of a permit will reduce the effects of uncertainty about future requirements because it tends to allow a more complete amortization of existing or newly installed equipment. With a short permit life, an operator must worry about how the requirements will change when the permit expires, particularly in view of the ratchet effect.

Federal water pollution permits for existing sources have a term of five years, while for new sources the term is ten years. There is evidence that some plants are attempting to have their sources classified as new sources, even though that designation subjects them to more stringent effluent standards (new source standards rather than best practicable technology) because they are willing to trade increased certainty for the increased costs of more stringent requirements.[38]

Improve Coordination with Other Federal and State Policies

At present, new industrial projects are subject to a wide array of environmental statutes besides the Clean Air and Clean Water acts.[39] The individual impact of any one of these statutes on business, much less the cumulative effects of all of them, could be substantial. It would be useful if the agencies administering these statutes could co-ordinate their efforts to ensure that this burden is no worse than necessary. Quarles suggests that one of the most difficult tasks for a businessman—especially a small businessman—is to find out precisely what kinds of regulations can affect him. This task becomes more difficult as new statutes are enacted or regulations issued. As Quarles points out,

> [A]lthough substantial considerations of public policy support the position that some system of government review should precede industrial decisions having major impacts on public values affecting

---

38. J. Quarles, *supra* note 11, at 25.

39. Examples include the National Environmental Policy Act, 42 U.S.C. §§ 4321-4374 (1976), the Endangered Species Act, 16 U.S.C. §§ 1531-1543 (1976), the Antiquities Act, 16 U.S.C. §§ 431-433 (1976), the Coastal Zone Management Act, 16 U.S.C. §§ 1451-1464, the Resource Conservation and Recovery Act, 42 U.S.C. §§ 6901-6987 (1976), and the Toxic Substance Control Act, 15 U.S.C. §§ 2601-2626 (1976). There is also a mass of legislation designed to advance other policy goals, such as worker health and safety, antitrust, energy conservation, coal conversion, and so on.

the environmental and natural resources, the current system of numerous single-purpose reviews, each conducted separately and according to its own timetable, is not the best solution. Appropriate environmental tradeoffs are difficult to make under the current framework; unnecessary paperwork and administrative burdens are virtually inevitable; and unduly long delays in reaching a final government decision are highly likely.[40]

Several measures could be taken to help streamline the permitting process. A regulatory clearinghouse, where a developer can find out the permits required for particular projects, might be useful. Another possibility would be to create an agency which would help secure the permits. Most important, a "one-stop" permitting process could be initiated, although this is not as simple as it might appear. The requirements of the various environmental statutes constrain the extent of possible consolidation. A one-stop process would also require much more cooperation and communication among disparate government agencies whose goals may conflict.

The Environmental Protection Agency began the complex and difficult task of consolidating permits in 1978. Over a year ago, two task forces were established: the New Source Review Task Force and the EPA Permit Consolidation Task Force. Among other things, the former recommended the designation of a new source facilitator/expediter in each region, so that a prospective applicant could go to one place in the agency to determine the requirements it would have to meet.[41]

The Permit Consolidation Task Force recently issued regulations which offer a single permit form to be used for simultaneous application and review of several EPA permits.[42] Definitions and program requirements have been made more uniform and a series of booklets on the regulations addressing the concerns of particular users will be issued.

The Environmental Protection Agency is also involved with expediting energy projects through its Energy Mobilization Task Force and developing a more efficient format for handling the environmental impact requirements of the National Environmental Protection Act. Thus the problem of duplicate, conflicting, and above all, cumulative permit requirements is well recognized within EPA, but numerous opportunities still exist for further consolidation of interagency permits.

---

40. J. Quarles, *supra* note 11, at 4.

41. EPA Consolidated Permit Regulations, 44 Fed. Reg. 34,244 (1978).

42. In response to concern that environmental groups will find it more difficult to challenge a consolidated permit, procedures for public hearings, evidentiary hearings, and nonadversary hearings are built into the process.

Reforms that streamline permit procedures will necessarily reduce opportunities for environmental and other citizens' groups to delay or alter projects. That is why the reforms will be so difficult to implement. Nevertheless, there may be some scope for shortening the time spent negotiating without compromising substance.

Cost-effectiveness Standards

As noted earlier, technology-based standards can impose very different marginal abatement costs for different industrial categories, resulting in losses in economic efficiency unless damages vary in the same way. One way of dealing with this problem in a regulatory framework is to set standards which equalize marginal abatement costs and thereby minimize the costs of obtaining the resulting reduction in aggregate emissions. There are three problems with this approach, however. The first is the designation of the marginal cost target, or "benchmark." There is no obvious connection between any benchmark and the resulting levels of environmental quality. The second problem is dividing the industry so that firms with similar abatement cost functions are in the same category. The third problem is that finding the standard corresponding to the benchmark entails construction of detailed marginal abatement cost functions in each industrial category. The more finely an industry is divided to obtain homogeneity, the more work is required to construct cost functions.

A version of this policy tool surfaced in the Clean Water Act of 1977.[43] To reduce the differences in marginal compliance costs of meeting best conventional technology, Congress designated the marginal cost per unit biological oxygen demand (BOD) removed by municipal waste treatment as a cost ceiling. Marginal costs above the ceiling for a subcategory presumably would provide grounds for EPA to lessen the subcategory's BCT standards. Marginal costs less than the ceiling would mean that the compliance costs were "reasonable." Thus Congress settled by legislative fiat the problem of setting the benchmark—at least in theory.[44] It is still too early to tell how this process will work out in practice.

---

43. 33 U.S.C. § 1314(b)(4)(B) (Supp. II 1978).

44. The initial EPA estimate of municipal marginal treatment costs of conventional pollutants was $1.15/lb. of BOD removed. The Council on Wage and Price Stability (COWPS) challenged EPA's estimates and methodology while issuing a benchmark range of its own. COWPS found marginal costs from $0.31 to $0.82 per pound of BOD removed depending on assumptions about the proper form of the abatement cost function and correcting for differences in plant performance variables. EPA responded that the wide variability of costs made any benchmark open to criticism. *See* A. Fraas & V. Munley, Municipal Wastewater Treatment Costs (Sept. 1980) (report to Council on Wage and Price Stability, Washington, D.C.).

Perhaps the greatest benefit from the implementation of cost-effectiveness standards for best conventional technology will be in setting precedents. In establishing limits for best available technology, a convenient benchmark marginal cost is unlikely to be available for the myriad nonconventional and toxic pollutants. But the principle of cutting down the variance of marginal abatement costs for a given pollutant over all affected sectors is worth serious consideration in future rulemaking.

Innovation Waivers

In amendments to both the Clean Air and Clean Water acts, the debilitating effects of technology-based standards on abatement innovation were recognized and legislative adjustments were introduced. In the Clean Air Act Amendments, firms experimenting with innovative abatement methods were given additional time to comply with the standards. However, with "innovation" never defined and poor agency support, the program has been limping along.[45] At present, a regulation is being drawn up to grant compliance delays for innovations under the Clean Water Act Amendments.[46] The statutory limit of a three-year extension is too short a period to stimulate anything but off-the-shelf technology. The inclusion, however, of process innovations in the "innovation" definition and support for the regulation within EPA should make it more successful than its counterpart in the air program. Still, if the program fails to provide additional compliance time for firms with innovative technologies that fail, the risks of innovating may still outweigh expected gains.

SUBSTANTIVE REFORMS

The procedural reforms discussed in the previous section center on changes in rulemaking or implementation that do not challenge the central place of technology-based standards in water and air pollution control policies. Certain substantive reforms, however, have begun to supplant the technology-based approach in state implementation plans and are on the drawing board in the water program at EPA.

There are powerful economic reasons for supporting economic incentive-based reforms over technology-based standards. Nevertheless,

---

45. J. Evans, Opportunities for Innovation: Administration of Section 111(j) and 113 (d)(4) of the CAA and Industry's Development of Innovative Control Technologies (Jan. 1980) (report of Performance Development Institute for U.S. Department of Commerce, Washington).

46. *See* A. Krupnick & D. Yardas, An Economic Analysis of an Innovation Waiver Policy under the Clean Water Act Amendments of 1977 (Dec. 1980) (report to Office of Planning and Evaluation, U.S. Environmental Protection Agency, Washington, D.C.).

the interest in these reforms owes more to the practical problems created by certain features of the Clean Air Act than to increased awareness of economic principles on the part of public officials and industry.[47] For areas in nonattainment, industrial growth has been effectively halted unless newcomers or expanding firms can secure emission reductions from an existing source or unless the state forces existing firms to roll back emissions to create a "margin for growth." In PSD areas, growth has also been limited because of requirements on emissions from new or expanding firms. Incentive-based policies can reduce both the roadblocks to growth and the compliance burden on existing firms. Also, some offices in EPA view these policies as a better means of fostering abatement innovations than through continuously redefining best available technology.

Bubbles, Banking, and Offsets

The details of these policies have been changing so rapidly that only their general characteristics are described below. Basically, they all involve shifting the clean-up burden toward sources with lower abatement costs and away from those with higher abatement costs. Thus, the aggregate compliance costs of meeting a standard can be reduced while maintaining or improving ambient quality. Firms have incentives to find the cheapest source to control even if the control involves a reallocation of abatement activity within the firm, an innovation, or the purchase of emission reductions from another firm.

Historically, offsets are EPA's first attempt to reduce compliance costs through reallocating the clean-up burden. New or expanding firms in a nonattainment area are required to install advanced treatment technology and secure emission reductions from other polluters in the area in excess of their own emissions.[48] The net effect of this policy is to allow for growth in nonattainment areas, while reducing air pollution and compliance costs. It also gives existing firms an incentive to find cheaper means of controlling their pollution. A more recent policy innovation allows firms that reduce emissions below their permit level to "bank" these emissions for use in their future expansion or to sell them to a new or expanding firm as an offset.

The bubble policy that was announced in December 1979 permits all of the stacks in a plant to be considered as one stack.[49] This pol-

---

47. In addition, Congress created the opportunity for these reforms in both the CAA and its amendments.

48. *See* 42 U.S.C. § 7503 (Supp. II 1978).

49. EPA's bubble policy was affirmed in *Alabama Power Co. v. Castle*, 636 F.2d 323 (D.C. Cir. 1979). The policy is codified in 40 C.F.R. §§ 51.24(b)(2) and 52.21(b)(2) (1978).

icy allows controls to be relaxed at those stacks where abatement costs are high and tightened at those stacks where control is cheaper. It is thus much like an offset transaction taking place within a firm. Recently, the policy has been broadened so that even plants with different owners and at different locations can use the bubble policy so long as air quality is not degraded.

Innovations that reduce emissions or costs may be stimulated under any of these programs because emission reductions resulting from these innovations can be sold, held for later use, or used to offset an increase in emissions elsewhere in a plant. In addition, should these reforms reduce uncertainty and other regulatory burdens, long-term investments and associated innovation prospects may be enhanced.

Experience

The Environmental Protection Agency claims that 650 documented offsets have taken place since January 1977.[50] Most of these were internal offsets—where an expansion of emissions at one source was more than compensated by a decrease in emissions from another source owned by the same firm (e.g., closing one plant and rebuilding another at the same site).

External offset transactions between two or more firms are not yet common. Those external offsets that have occurred may not be typical of future offsets because they involve once-and-for-all emission reductions, such as the substitution of water-based for oil-based asphalt by a state highway authority.[51]

Experience with bubbles and banking is very limited. The first bubble application was approved in November 1980, when an electric utility proposed to substitute high for low sulfur coal at one plant while burning natural gas instead of low sulfur coal at another plant. Sulfur dioxide emissions should fall overall, with savings of $27 mil-

---

50. U.S. Environmental Protection Agency, Controlled Trading: A Generic Term (paper distributed at EPA conference on regulatory reform, Washington, D.C., September 18-19, 1980).

51. One much publicized case involved a new General Motors plant and offsets obtained from local oil companies in Shreveport, Louisiana, and Oklahoma City. As a result of these transactions engineered by local Chambers of Commerce in both areas, GM built a $400 million plant employing several thousand people. However, not only were the offsets given at no cost, so the incentive for locating the cheapest sources didn't exist, but most of the offsets were only on paper. The oil companies were voluntarily abating pollution they would have been required to abate two years later (under a ruling being discussed at that time). Also, they were going to make some of the adjustments on their own for economic reasons. *See* R. LIROFF, AIR POLLUTION OFFSETS: TRADING, SELLING, AND BANKING (1980).

lion per year. Over 40 companies are developing bubble applications, showing savings of several million dollars each in either capital or operating costs.[52] Banking programs have recently begun in San Francisco, Puget Sound, and Louisville, but few transactions have taken place. Thirty states are formally considering the banking approach.[53]

Problems

Although it is certainly too early to make solid judgments on the viability of these programs and their macroeconomic impacts, it is not surprising that the initial experience has been mixed. A major problem lies in the conservatism of firm managers who may fear that these policies will be followed in short order by others. New policies may have contradictory requirements that leave them stuck with valueless banked emissions and converted boilers that would need to be reconverted. Another problem is the administrative obstacles and high cost of obtaining bubbles and banking emissions. Only firms in compliance may apply, and a SIP revision is required for every bubble —a lengthy and nonroutine process.[54]

The Environmental Protection Agency is working to reduce regulatory uncertainties and simplify some administrative procedures, but the policies still have basic problems. First, the scope for trading offsets is limited by the technology requirements on new and existing sources. New or expanding firms must still install expensive abatement technologies. Thus, offset trading and the cost savings that go with it involve only the relatively small amount of emissions not treated by this technology. Existing sellers of offsets also have technology-based standards to meet.[55] Further, firms that are likely to be facing the largest abatement costs are those excluded from these plans—namely, those firms not in compliance. While an equity case can certainly be made for treating recalcitrant firms differently from

---

52. U.S. Environmental Protection Agency, *The Bubble Clearinghouse* (EPA Newsletter-Dec. 1980).

53. The performance of the bank in Puget Sound cannot yet be evaluated because it is too new, but over 90 requests for credits have been received. In San Francisco there exists an informal bank for emission credits deposited by a firm for its future use, and a formal bank where credits are available for sale to other firms. Participation in the informal bank has been high because many firms which had installed more strict controls than necessary prior to the bank's operation were "grandfathered" in. No deposits to the formal bank have been made as yet. In Louisville, the 20 deposits resulted mainly from shut-downs. Personal communication with Charles Bausell, economist, General Accounting Office, Washington, D.C. (Dec. 12, 1980).

54. New rules put into effect recently by EPA, the so-called "generic" bubble policy, waive the SIP revision rule if certain conditions are met. *See Inside EPA: Weekly Report* (Dec. 5, 1980).

55. These standards are termed Reasonably Available Control Technologies (RACT).

those cooperating with clean-up efforts, there would likely be efficiency gains if such firms were included.[56]

Another problem plaguing these policy initiatives is the high transaction costs involved in finding offset or bubble partners. Few seekers of offsets have actually paid another firm to reduce its emissions so that the firm could move in or expand. The SOHIO case in California is an example of an attempted offset reportedly beset by delay and strategic behavior on the part of suppliers of potential offsets.[57] Moreover, the volume of offsets, formal emission deposits, and multifirm bubble opportunities has not been sufficient to facilitate the development of a market. The problem is classically circular: thin markets generate little profit for middlemen, so they don't participate. Without middlemen the market stays thin.

Among other problems, monitoring is particularly vexing. The approval of bubbles and offsets requires air diffusion modeling to prove nondegradation of air quality under certain conditions. Much disagreement exists on the capabilities of air quality models, their consistency with one another, their appropriateness in various situations, and so on. Until agreement is reached, the required use of such models will add to the uncertainty surrounding these policies and restrict participation.

Turning to macroeconomic effects, well-functioning offset, bubble, and banking systems could improve the allocation of resources, increase productivity and innovation, and reduce inflation. But a poorly functioning offset program will tend to restrict entry of new sources into nonattainment areas and discourage the expansion of existing plants. Also, because most nonattainment areas contain large cities with high unemployment, an unworkable offset program could seriously undermine attempts to reduce the rate of unemployment. Finally, problems in implementing these programs and in relaxing the vast array of conditions burdening banking and bubble programs may sour industry and regulatory authorities on other incentive approaches to pollution control.

Marketable Pollution Permits

The marketable pollution permit (MPP) approach to controlling pollution is an idea first advanced by Dales in 1968 as an alternative to effluent taxes. Until recently, this idea generated little but aca-

---

56. Recalcitrant firms selling offsets would then be given credit for emission reductions they should have made.

57. *See* CONGRESSIONAL RESEARCH SERVICE, *supra* note 24, at 105-32.

demic interest.[58] It wasn't until the application and elaboration of the offset policy that EPA began to consider buying and selling pollution permits. Now, marketable permits are seen as the final step in a progression that includes the bubble and banking policies discussed earlier.

Moving to a full marketable permit system in nonattainment areas would first involve the elimination of all technology-based emission standards. In addition, the banking, bubble and offset policies, together with associated administrative procedures (e.g., revisions of state implementation plans), would be combined and simplified. In PSD areas, the lack of an offset policy means that greater institutional changes would be required. Nonetheless, with ambient standards tighter than the national ambient standards, a marketable permit system is perfectly compatible with prevention of significant deterioration.

Two general types of marketable permit systems can be envisioned, one based on emission permits and another on ambient permits.[59] Where ambient conditions are relatively insensitive to polluter location—chlorofluoromethane emissions may be an example—a system where permits are defined in terms of allowable emissions may work well. Thus, a firm in California could sell its right to emit 100 pounds of Freon to a firm in New York without a change in the effect of the Freon on stratospheric ozone.

Where the location of the source matters, as is the case with NO_x or particulates, the authority could issue permits allowing the source to have some specified effect on ambient pollutant concentrations at particular receptor points. These permits would also contain information to convert concentrations to allowable emissions. When concentration permits are traded between firms, allowable emissions would need to be adjusted because the emissions value of a right to degrade air at a receptor by one unit depends on the location of the buyer and seller relative to the receptor.[60]

---

58. *See* J. DALES, POLLUTION, PROPERTY, AND PRICES (1968); D. Montgomery, *Markets in Licenses and Efficient Pollution Control Programs*, 5 J. ECON. THEORY 395 (1972); T. Tietenberg, The Design of Property Rights for Air Pollution Control, 22 PUB. POL'Y 275 (1974).

59. A. Krupnick & W. Oates, On the Design of a Market For Air Pollution Permits: The Spatial Problem (July 1980) (paper presented at Western Economics Association Meeting, San Diego, Calif.).

60. This information is embodied in a ratio of transfer coefficients (termed exchange rates), $\frac{T_{ij}}{T_{kj}}$, where T_{ij} is the contribution of a source at location i per unit of emissions to the concentration of a pollutant at receptor j. *See* D. Montgomery, *supra* note 58, for more on this point.

If ambient standards are to be met at all points, the ambient permit system must be complex, requiring a firm to hold a portfolio of permits covering each receptor point.[61] In contrast, the emission system requires holding only one type of permit. Yet, the simplicity of the latter system comes at the cost of uncertainty over meeting ambient standards and in a loss of efficiency. A study of the abatement cost of meeting a hypothetical short-term NO_x standard in the Chicago area indicates that the compliance costs may be up to ten times higher with a uniform rather than a fully spatially differentiated market permit (or effluent fee) system.[62] For longer term standards, different pollutants, or other locations, the cost savings may be less. In any case, balancing the costs and benefits of greater spatial differentiation can provide guidance about the type of system to adopt.

The theoretical advantages of marketable pollution permit systems may be compromised by uncertainty created by two implementation problems.[63] First, firms must have confidence regarding the future behavior of the government. Unless discharge permits are treated as property rights, entitled to the same constitutional guarantees as other property, firms would face the uncertainty of having their permits revoked or redefined in the future. At the same time, when the government wishes to change the quantity of rights outstanding, it must do so in a way that minimizes market disruption.[64] Second, firms may face market uncertainty if the number of participants is too few. A potential buyer's fear that it will be unable to find a seller will itself tend to prevent trading, causing firms to hold their permits for future use rather than make them available to others. Strategic concerns may also hinder market development, i.e., a firm may have monopoly power and refuse to sell its permits to prevent entry or expansion by other firms.

In view of these shortcomings, it is clear that marketable permits will not be a panacea; the proper regulatory environment that would make these permit markets viable will not be easily or quickly

---

61. Since national ambient standards must be met at all points, in theory the portfolio would be infinitely large. In practice, receptor points in a given area could be sifted for hot spots. Then the overall airshed would be divided into markets, each with its own hot spot. Exchange rates would be computed from these receptor points.

62. U.S. ENVT'L PROTECTION AGENCY & COUNCIL OF ECONOMIC ADVISERS, AN ANALYSIS OF MARKET INCENTIVE TO CONTROL STATIONARY SOURCE NO_x EMISSIONS (Draft–Oct. 1980).

63. Other implementation issues concern the distribution of permits, their terms, participation by citizen groups and other third parties, verification, and enforcement. *See* S. Rose-Ackerman, *Market Models for Water Pollution Control: Their Strengths and Weaknesses*, 25 PUB. POL'Y 383 (1977), for a discussion of implementation issues.

64. The analogy to government behavior with strategic metal or petroleum reserves is instructive here.

achieved. The macroeconomic effects associated with reduced compliance costs and increased innovation may therefore be slow in coming. Present regulatory uncertainty caused by changes in technology-based stndards may only be replaced by a different kind of uncertainty—that associated with the operation of the permit markets.

Effluent Charges

No discussion of environmental policy options would be complete without mention of effluent fees, but because this approach is already the subject of a vast literature, we will be brief.[65] Under an effluent fee policy, each discharger must pay a fee or tax for each unit of pollution discharged. By forcing firms to internalize heretofore external costs, this fee provides an incentive for pollution abatement.

In theory, effluent fees share with marketable permits two important advantages over technology-based standards. First, with either system, an aggregate pollution discharge target can be met at least cost. Under a uniform effluent fee, each plant would reduce its pollution discharge until the marginal cost of further abatement equaled the fee. Most of the abating would be done by those for whom it was least expensive.[66] In addition, fees offer an important long-term advantage over standards; every discharger has an incentive to search for both pollution-reducing and cost-reducing abatement innovations. As noted earlier, effluent standards encourage only innovations that reduce cost.

Effluent fees also enjoy important advantages over marketable permits. Because the fee approach does not require the operation of a market, the problems of establishing a market, of market thinness, and of monopoly power discussed earlier are avoided. In addition, an effluent fee avoids the rigid constraints on growth imposed by a too-restrictive permit system because the level of the fee places a ceiling on marginal abatement costs.

Unfortunately, however, effluent fees have their own unique disadvantages.[67] One is the obverse of the problem mentioned in the preceding paragraph. In an expanding economy, while marketable permits risk imposing heavier than optimal abatement costs, constant effluent fees risk deteriorating environmental quality. Second, effluent fees are emasculated through inflation.

---

65. *See, e.g.,* W. BAUMOL & W. OATES, THE THEORY OF ENVIRONMENTAL POLICY (1975).

66. However, environmental quality depends not only on the sum of pollution discharges, but on their spatial and temporal patterns. For this reason a nonuniform fee—one depending on the location of the discharger—may be less costly.

67. For further discussion see Rose-Ackerman, *Effluent Charges: A Critique,* 6 CAN. J. ECON. 512 (1973).

A third problem of effluent fees is the disposition of the collected revenues. The cost of an effluent charge policy to a firm includes not only the cost of abatement but also the taxes it pays on its remaining discharges. Unless these transfer payments are returned to industry, the total cost of an effluent charge system to the producing sector may be greater than under an effluent standards policy, even though the abatement cost is less.[68]

Finally, it is difficult to determine what the effects of a given fee structure on ambient environmental quality will be. Achieving an ambient quality objective with effluent fees requires fairly detailed knowledge of the abatement cost functions of all dischargers and the "transfer coefficients" between each discharger and the different areas of the receiving medium. Only the latter is required for either marketable permits or effluent standards. To remedy this problem, some writers have suggested a trial-and-error approach or a "self-adjusting" charge. In either case, the fee would initially be set at a low level and would increase annually until the desired ambient conditions were met. This approach might work with a uniform charge, but if the fee is spatially differentiated and some areas exceed the ambient objective and other areas fail to meet it, it would be virtually impossible to know how to adjust the fee structure. This problem would be especially difficult in an area undergoing rapid economic growth.

CONCLUSION

The high costs and limited success of the air and water pollution policies formulated in the early 1970s have given impetus to a search for reform. Most of the suggested reforms discussed above have been promoted either to remove procedural obstacles to plant expansion or to replace the current command-and-control approach to regulation with economic incentives. Their proponents see these reforms as the means to a considerable reduction in the cost of environmental policy, with little, if any, sacrifice in environmental quality. At the same time, many of these ideas will be strenuously opposed by environmentalists, who generally fear that any change in the status quo will represent a retreat in the nation's commitment to environmental quality.

The effects of these reforms may not be nearly as disastrous as op-

---

68. E. Brill, C. Revelle & J. Liebman, *An Effluent Charge Schedule: Cost, Financial Burden and Punitive Effects*, 15 WATER RES. RESEARCH 993 (1979). Transfer payments would need to be returned to industry in such a way that incentives to abate are left undisturbed.

ponents fear. There is little in them that is inherently hostile to environmental quality. Indeed, if these policy instruments can achieve given levels of environmental quality at lower economic cost, the tension that certainly now exists between the goals of environmental quality and economic growth will be reduced. In other words, cost-effective policy instruments are also environmentally benign.

However, the expectations of the benefit to be derived from any of the alternatives need to be tempered. Some of the difficulties of the current approach are not corrected by any of the reforms discussed here, and may well be inevitable regardless of policy. One of these is the need for source surveillance. Accurate information about what sources are actually discharging is necessary to determine whether effluent standards or permit conditions are being complied with, and to calculate each plant's effluent charge payment. However, surveillance is expensive and for this reason has hitherto been infrequent. Therefore, we do not really know the extent to which existing permits or standards are being violated, although some empirical work suggests that it is substantial.[69]

Another difficulty with current policy that is not easily handled by the reforms we have discussed is the spatial problem. Every imaginable pollution control policy works immeasurably better for those pollution problems which are not location-specific. Unfortunately, few problems fall into this category.

A third element common to all policies is the importance of politics. Attempts to remove political considerations from environmental policy-making have been prominent ever since environmental concerns first arose. For example, the desire to put environmental concerns above politics probably contributed to Congress' initial embrace of the technology-based approach; it was hoped that these standards could be based purely on technical decisions made by disinterested experts at EPA. We know now that enough ambiguity was written into the Clean Air Act and the Federal Water Pollution Control Act to allow extensive room for negotiation between EPA and affected industries, as well as plenty of opportunities to apply political pressure. These opportunities will almost surely be just as important for any other policy instrument.[70] Environmental decisions *are* political, of course, because alternative policies or programs have different dis-

---

69. W. Harrington, THE REGULATORY APPROACH TO AIR QUALITY MANAGEMENT: A CASE STUDY OF NEW MEXICO (1981).

70. C. Russell, *What Can We Get From Effluent Charges*, 5 POL'Y ANALYSIS 155 (1979), argues that an effluent charge system will be subject to the same political influences as the current regulatory approach.

tributional consequences. What we rather disparagingly call "politics" is really the process by which various parties exercise their rights to be heard and to petition for a redress of grievances. Choice of policy instrument will not affect this fact, inconvenient though it may be.

Finally, much of the uncertainty that is said to dampen the entrepreneurial spirit may be an inevitable consequence of environmental policy. One reason environmental regulation imposes so much uncertainty on the economy is that so little is known about the health and ecological effects of pollution, especially trace amounts of toxic materials. Removing regulatory barriers to economic growth does not eliminate this uncertainty; rather it shifts the burden of risk to the environment.

We insert these notes of caution, not because we think that environmental policy reform is hopeless. On the contrary, the alternatives discussed here, especially those involving economic incentives, offer much promise. However, nothing would destroy that promise with greater sureness than a backlash caused by unfulfilled expectations.

Long-Run Effects of Environmental Regulation

RONALD G. RIDKER and WILLIAM D. WATSON*

INTRODUCTION

The preceding papers in this volume have considered the effects of environmental regulation on the economy during the past and into the near future. However, it is also important to study the longer run as well as the shorter run implications of such regulations. First, there may be some consequences too small or subtle to worry about in the short run but which may have significant cumulative effects over several decades. Second, environmental policies appropriate for the next few years may require investments and institutional arrangements that are inappropriate from a longer term perspective. This paper attempts to illustrate these points by examining the relationship between the generation of pollutants, environmental regulation, and economic growth over a fifty-year period. In doing so, we draw upon the results of our recent and highly detailed study of these issues.[1]

Long-run economic analysis is very difficult and often quite different from shorter run analysis. First, the nature and determinants of environmental problems are frequently different in the long run as opposed to the short run. For example, during the next five years or so, any economic problems associated with regulation must focus on meeting compliance requirements. Over this five-year period, the effects of changes in the size and composition of the population, in per capita incomes, tastes, technology, and in the nature of economic activities will not be significant. But as the time horizon is lengthened, these more fundamental determinants of economic growth and environmental quality grow in importance.

Long-run analysis is difficult for another reason. As income increases and tastes and technology change over time, the composition of output will change. Because each sector of the economy generates

*Ronald G. Ridker is a senior economist in the Policy Planning Divison of the World Bank. He is on leave from his position as a senior fellow in the Renewable Resources Division, Resources for the Future. William Watson is an economist in the Programs Office of the United States Geological Survey.

1. R. RIDKER & W. WATSON, TO CHOOSE A FUTURE: RESOURCES AND ENVIRONMENTAL CONSEQUENCES OF ALTERNATIVE GROWTH PATHS (1980). Portions of this paper are adapted from this volume; other portions utilized unpublished materials from the underlying study.

a different mix of pollutants and because technological change as well as other factors affect these mixes, the composition of pollutants cannot be expected to remain the same or to maintain the same relationship to aggregate output as they have in the past. In addition, changes in the geographic distribution of population and economic activities can have significant environmental impacts in the long run. In these circumstances, the results of aggregate analysis may be misleading. Despite its greater cost, data requirements, and analytical complexity, a substantial amount of disaggregation is necessary in long-run analyses even if interest is focused on only a few aggregates.

On top of these complexities, there are a vast number of interdependencies and feedbacks to reckon with. If access to one form of energy is restricted, then other forms may be substituted (for example, coal for oil). If restrictions are placed on the use of the automobile, other forms of transportation, with their own array of environmental problems, might become attractive. If wastes are not emitted into the air, they will show up in liquid or solid form. If environmental regulations on some sectors become too costly to meet, the economic activities involved may be moved or substitutes for their output may be found. In truth, everything—from migration patterns and attitudes toward work to economic and political developments in the rest of the world—is related to everything else and these relationships can change in important ways in coming decades.

There is no way any one study can account adequately for all these complexities. As a consequence, our results are limited in several senses. First, our results cannot be considered unconditional forecasts of the future. All we can do is spell out some of the implications of different courses of actions when they occur within specific contexts. Thus, our results cannot be used intelligently to evaluate alternative courses of action without an understanding of all the conditions assumed in their development. While the overall nature of these conditions can be presented in this brief paper, the reader must refer to our longer study for more details.[2]

Second, the analysis is limited mainly to what we call the mass pollutants. These pollutants, referred to in the air and water pollution control regulations as "criteria" air pollutants and "conventional" water pollutants, have been the primary objects of concern in environmental regulations during the past decade. Other environmental problems, many of which will become more important in the future, are briefly discussed in the concluding section.

Third, the focus in our analysis is on direct and indirect effects

---

2. *Id.*

that can be derived from input-output analysis supplemented by regional analysis and efforts to quantify the direct benefits and costs of different hypothetical levels of environmental controls. The implications of environmental regulations for other social and political issues (for example, land use planning and the distribution of gains and losses from controlling pollution) that might affect the economy are not studied.

METHODOLOGY

Our analysis involves five steps: (1) projecting national economic activity, abatement costs, and point source pollution levels; (2) assigning pollutants from point sources to regions; (3) estimating pollutants from regional transportation, urban runoff, agricultural, mining, and other nonpoint sources; (4) translating estimated pollutant generation into regional ambient air and water pollution concentrations; and (5) estimating regional air and water pollution damage as a function of regional ambient conditions. The appendix discusses the estimating methods used in the various steps.

Three alternative and hypothetical national pollution control policies are simulated in this paper: we refer to them as strict, relaxed, and cost minimizing. The first two (see Table 1) reflect our assessment of a possible range of future EPA regulations, starting from a base of 1975. The strict case is not unlike currently legislated federal air and water regulations; however, we have not assumed that all discharges to water will be eliminated by 1985; nor do we take account of the shift in the policy focus from conventional to toxic water pollutants. The relaxed control policy more nearly approximates actual practice in U.S. environmental policy although it includes weaker rules and allows more time for compliance. In our cost-minimizing case, controls are set at the point where the sum of expected pollution control and damage costs is a minimum.

THE NATIONAL ECONOMY

The basic quantitative assumptions that underlie our analysis are given in Table 2. As can be seen, this scenario projects that real GNP will double between 1975 and 2000 and increase another 60 percent in the subsequent twenty-five years. These increases represent substantial slowdowns from comparable periods before 1975 and result from declines in population and labor force growth rates, changes in labor productivity arising from shifts in the composition of the labor force and of output, and a number of transitional factors related to higher energy prices and environmental clean-up costs. Our assumed

TABLE 1

STRICT AND RELAXED POLLUTION CONTROL POLICIES

Element and Policy	Standards
Water	
Strict	Conventional treatment technology in 1977, advanced treatment technology in 1983.
Relaxed	Conventional treatment technology in 1980, advanced treatment technology for construction begun on or after 1990.
Air—Mobile sources	
Strict	Federal standards for new cars starting in 1978
Relaxed	Federal standards for new cars starting in 1978, *plus* less stringent controls in the period after 2000.
Air—Stationary sources	
Strict	Conventional treatment technology standards by 1977, advanced treatment technology standards for construction begun on or after 1980 *except* control of sulfur oxide for electric utilities to be implemented immediately for high-sulfur fuels and after 1980 for all fuels.
Relaxed	Conventional treatment technology standards by 1978; advanced treatment technology standards for construction begun on or after 1983 *except* control of sulfur oxide for electric utilities starting in 1976 for high-sulfur fuels and for all fuels by 1990, *plus* some relaxation in standards for some pollutants in some sectors.

rate of economic growth may be too high. The lower rates experienced in the 1970s may be more typical. On the other hand, it may be too low if we have underestimated the rate of growth of the labor force.

The fraction of GNP that is comprised of government expenditures declines over this projection period, primarily because we assume that the defense, education, and public construction shares of GNP will decline. We assume defense to be like expenditures on insurance, which rise less than proportionately to income; the other sectors are expected to decline because of such factors as a decline in population growth and the completion of the federal highway system. Our projected decline in the government's share of GNP does not necessarily indicate a reduction in the economic importance of this sector because its size is not defined to include transfer payments which may continue to grow over time. Indeed, this growth in transfers partly accounts for the rise in the share of GNP derived from personal consumption expenditures over time. The share of invest-

TABLE 2

UNDERLYING POPULATION AND ECONOMIC PROJECTIONS

	1975	1985	2000	2025
Population (millions)	213.9	230.9	250.7	264.9
Labor force (millions)	93.8	108.2	122.3	125.1
GNP (billions 1971$)	1,108	1,589	2,385	3,859
GNP per capita (1971$)	5,180	6,921	9,513	14,568
Private consumption per capita (1971$)	3,202	4,172	6,002	9,651
Percentage of GNP				
Private consumption	61.8	60.6	63.1	66.3
Private investment	14.8	19.1	17.2	17.0
Government expenditure	21.4	20.1	19.6	17.6
Net exports	2.0	0.2	0.1	0.8

ment (private and public and inventory charge) also increases up to about 1990, after which it declines slightly, but never to the 1975 level. A significant portion of this increase results from a growing need to replace old capital equipment in some heavy industries and increased expenditures on energy-producing, energy-saving, and pollution-abating equipment, most of which must be made in the 1980s.

Despite these changes, the composition of output is only modestly affected. Agriculture, mining, and construction continue their slow decline; manufacturing just holds its own (with steel becoming less important and industrial chemicals somewhat more important) and other sectors, such as the personal services, increase their shares. However, all these changes are small and slow.

Some modest changes in the geographic location of populations and economic activities are also assumed. For example, shifts of population and economic activity to the "sun belt" states are continued. Except for primary energy production (which must be located close to energy sources) and nuclear power production (which has other site criteria), historical trends are continued, but at increasingly dampened rates of change. Again, for the most part these changes are small and gradual.

EMISSIONS AND CONCENTRATION LEVELS

Table 3 indicates national emissions levels for various pollutants in 1975 and in future years given this scenario for national economic growth. Gross emissions indicate the levels that would occur in the

TABLE 3

NATIONAL EMISSIONS FOR ALTERNATIVE POLICIES
(millions of tons)

Emission and policy[a]	1975	1985	2000	2025
Particulate matter (PM)				
Gross[b]	98.0	154.4	151.0	227.6
Net R	24.2	12.2	2.4	2.0
S	19.5	2.8	1.8	1.4
M	6.7	5.8	2.0	1.8
Sulfur oxides (SO_x)				
Gross	49.7	63.0	53.1	72.1
Net R	37.6	40.0	24.8	18.1
S	32.2	17.0	9.3	6.7
M	15.6	8.9	9.1	10.6
Nitrogen oxides (NO_x)				
Gross	18.7	21.5	16.4	23.1
Net R	18.5	18.5	10.8	12.0
S	17.7	14.6	8.2	8.0
M	18.4	17.2	12.4	15.1
Hydrocarbons (HC)				
Gross	26.7	19.7	22.0	25.3
Net R	20.7	9.0	6.7	5.5
S	19.2	6.5	4.9	3.8
M	17.2	13.5	11.9	9.3
Carbon monoxide				
Gross	125.4	110.8	135.2	161.2
Net R	87.2	28.0	15.6	15.4
S	85.0	22.6	11.6	9.2
M	124.1	96.1	105.9	128.2
Biochemical oxygen demand (BOD)				
Gross	19.8	22.3	27.0	36.5
Net R	8.0	7.3	6.2	5.4
S	7.3	4.0	3.1	2.6
M	8.9	7.6	7.3	7.6
Chemical oxygen demand (COD)				
Gross	15.7	19.4	25.5	36.4
Net R	7.2	5.5	4.1	3.7
S	6.9	2.9	2.4	1.7
M	5.6	3.8	4.0	6.5
Suspended solids (SS)				
Gross	722.1	635.3	743.9	931.4
Net R	543.5	544.8	466.4	434.2
S	510.6	313.7	297.8	326.8
M	510.6	321.1	307.5	350.7
Dissolved solids (DS)				
Gross	361.7	334.3	401.6	512.5
Net R	296.0	307.0	212.0	196.0
S	282.2	149.6	139.8	150.5
M	282.1	152.5	146.1	159.8

TABLE 3 (continued)

Emission and policy[a]	1975	1985	2000	2025
Nutrients				
Gross	8.5	8.4	8.9	9.7
Net R	6.0	6.3	6.1	5.1
S	5.6	4.5	4.3	3.6
M	5.6	4.8	4.7	4.3
Other[c]				
Gross	5.9	6.9	8.9	11.7
Net R	4.8	4.0	2.3	1.7
S	4.8	1.8	1.2	1.4
M	4.7	2.0	1.3	2.0

[a]Emissions from point sources (industry, electric utilities, and municipal wastewater treatment plants); transportation sources; urban runoff; point emissions and sediment runoff from minerals, ore, and coal mining and milling; and sediment runoff from nonurban construction, forestry, and agriculture.

[b]Gross emissions from mining and nonpoint sources (other than agriculture and urban runoff) are calculated as emissions that would have occurred assuming 1975 control levels in every year after 1975. Gross emissions for agricultural nonpoint sources are emissions that would have occurred if emission control measures in effect in 1975 and subsequent years were to be removed. Gross emissions for point sources and urban runoff are discharges assuming no control in any year.

[c]Includes acids, bases, oils, grease, heavy metals, and pesticides. The heavy metals included here are for ore, coal, and minerals mining, forestry, and nonurban construction. Heavy metals for other sources (including industrial point sources) are included in the suspended and dissolved solids estimates.

absence of any pollution controls. Three different levels of net emissions are also presented, depending on the control policies assumed— R (relaxed), S (strict), and M (minimum cost). While gross emissions in our scenario grow significantly over time, net emissions generally decline, more rapidly under policy S than policy R. The timing of the declines is a reflection of the timing of introductions of policy changes (see Table 1). The minimum cost strategy generally produces emission levels between R and S. There are a few notable exceptions for which emissions under policy M are above both R and S. A plausible explanation is that in the case of those pollutants, society is willing to pay something extra to achieve a reduction in risks of experiencing above-average damage levels over a minimum-cost strategy. An alternative explanation is that the R and S controls are technology-based standards that give only partial consideration to cost impacts. Therefore, R or S can be expected to produce emissions that are different from M.

Table 4 indicates concentration levels likely to be experienced in certain regions (the 243 air quality control regions and 101 watersheds into which the country has been divided). The pattern is simi-

TABLE 4

REGIONAL AMBIENT POLLUTION CONCENTRATIONS FOR ALTERNATIVE POLICIES

Pollutant and policy	1975			1985			2000			2025		
	H	Mn	V	H	Mn	V	H	Mn	V	H	Mn	V
Particulate matter (PM) (μg/m³)[a]												
R	159.2	54.5	48	80.2	43.7	5	58.3	36.7	0	59.3	36.1	0
S	132.2	52.0	34	77.2	36.7	2	60.3	36.1	0	60.0	35.6	0
M	90.3	40.0	2	88.0	37.9	2	59.3	36.1	0	59.4	35.7	0
Sulfur oxides (SOₓ) (μg/m³)[b]												
R	140.4	12.4	36	151.4	10.6	29	88.1	6.8	2	154.3	5.3	3
S	171.3	11.9	37	127.4	6.7	8	71.1	4.5	0	68.2	3.7	0
M	81.4	6.5	1	78.9	4.5	0	53.0	4.4	0	70.0	4.2	0
Nitrogen oxides (NOₓ) (μg/m³)[c]												
R	108.3	26.7	2	98.7	26.2	0	62.8	23.3	0	60.7	22.2	0
S	108.3	26.5	2	84.4	25.3	1	53.8	22.7	0	46.7	21.6	0
M	108.3	26.7	2	96.7	25.8	8	82.9	24.3	1	60.8	22.8	0
Hydrocarbons (HC) (1975=100)[d]												
R	100.0	100.0		71.2	34.2		54.1	24.0		43.0	14.8	
S	116.2	105.2		53.0	34.7		39.0	24.3		28.1	13.2	
M	129.8	87.2		107.6	52.1		115.5	40.8		74.0	22.8	

	H	Mn	V	H	Mn	V	H	Mn	V
Carbon monoxide (CO) (mg/m³)[e]									
R	34.8	3.1	59	12.7	2.3	3	7.2	2.2	0
S	36.0	3.1	57	14.4	2.3	3	7.1	2.1	0
M	45.6	3.6	65	41.2	3.1	60	48.3	3.6	64
Water pollution (PDI index)[f]									
R	20.7	1.5	11	18.6	1.3	6	9.0	0.6	1
S	12.2	1.4	10	6.5	0.7	1	2.6	0.3	0
M	12.6	1.4	10	10.6	1.1	4	17.2	0.9	3

The figures in this table refer to 243 air quality control regions (AQCRs) and 101 watersheds.

Note: Column heading abbreviations are: H, highest concentration over all regions; Mn, median concentration over all regions; V, number of regions where indicated standard is violated.

[a] Annual average concentration; primary standard is 75 µg/m³.
[b] Annual average concentration; primary standard is 80 µg/m³.
[c] Annual average concentration; primary standard is 100 µg/m³.
[d] It is not possible to calculate violations for this measure.
[e] Eight-hour concentration; primary standard is 10 mg/m³.
[f] The PDI (prevalence, duration, intensity) index measures ambient water quality based upon expert judgment [J. B. Truitt, A. C. Johnson, W. D. Rowe, K. D. Feigner, and L. J. Manning, "Development of Water Quality Management Indices," *Water Resources Bulletin*, vol. 11, no. 3 (June, 1975)]. Violations are the number of watersheds with PDIs in excess of 5.35. This value is the average PDI in 1975 plus one standard error when policy R is in effect.

lar to that observed for emissions. Between 1975 and 1985 there are substantial declines in median levels and the number of regions in violation of standards under all policies. By 2000, with the exception of carbon monoxide under a least-cost policy, there is virtually no region remaining that is in violation of ambient standards, and by ratcheting up control levels to compensate for increasing gross emissions, this situation can be made to continue through 2025.

ABATEMENT COSTS

Table 5 presents the abatement costs which we have estimated to be incurred under the strict and relaxed standards through the year 2025. These are *not* unconditional forecasts of future abatement expenditures, even though we tried to make the 1975 levels comparable to reported actual expenditures. Since that time, federal air and water pollution control laws have changed in ways we have not attempted to incorporate. As can be seen, these costs rise more rapidly than GNP under both sets of standards. As a percentage of GNP, however, the costs are currently less than 2 percent and do not increase to more than 3 percent before 2020, and then only in the strict case.

However, this picture is somewhat misleading in two senses. As Figure 1 indicates, we assume that abatement expenditures are not spread smoothly over time. Under the strict policy, they rise rapidly from 1975 to a peak in 1979 of more than 2.6 percent and remain high until 1983, when they fall to 2.2 percent. This period, during which the majority of the legislated standards must be met, involves the most rapid rate of expansion of projected abatement expenditures during the fifty-year period covered by this study, and those expenditures explain a substantial portion of the increased requirements for environmental spending noted for this period. Thereafter, abatement expenditures grow more smoothly over time, except for several peaks and troughs that can be explained by the timing of additional regulations and equipment replacement cycles. Additional new source regulations for point sources are assumed to be imposed for the strict policy beginning in about the year 2000. In the case of relaxed policy, it is assumed that the additional new source standards are delayed until about the year 2010.

Parenthetically, it can also be noted that shifts in assumptions about population and economic growth rates (compare the alternative projections provided in Figure 1) do not appear to have as significant an impact on the percentage of GNP devoted to abatement as does a change in policy (compare the strict and relaxed standards in Table 5).

TABLE 5

PROJECTED ANNUALIZED ABATEMENT COSTS FOR SELECTED YEARS
(billions of 1971 dollars)

	Strict standards				Relaxed standards			
	1975[a]	1985	2000	2025	1975[a]	1985	2000	2025
Air pollution	4.1	14.3	20.5	36.1	3.5	11.1	17.0	30.1
Mobile	1.2	7.4	11.4	10.8	1.2	7.4	11.2	9.6
Electric utilities	1.1	3.4	3.2	3.7	1.0	1.4	1.4	3.3
Water pollution	9.3	27.6	36.3	86.8	7.7	17.2	23.4	52.3
Industrial point sources	4.9	13.4	17.4	57.1	4.7	8.4	13.4	38.8
Electric utilities	0.3	0.6	0.9	2.0	0.2	0.3	0.4	0.7
Municipal wastewater	3.7	12.4	16.3	25.9	2.8	7.7	8.2	11.3
Urban runoff	...	2.2	4.0	6.9	...	0.8	1.2	2.0
Nonpoint sources	...	2.2	2.4	2.3	...	0.2	1.2	1.5
Agricultural sediment	...	1.0	0.9	0.8	...	0	0	0
Construction sediment	...	0.4	0.3	0.4	...	0.2	0.3	0.4
Forestry sediment	...	0.1	0.2	0.4	...	0	0.2	0.4
Acid mine sediment	...	0.7	1.0	0.7	...	0	0.7	0.7
Thermal pollution	0.4	1.2	1.7	1.8	0.1	0	1.3	1.4
Solid waste	0.6	1.1	1.7	2.3	0.6	0.8	1.7	2.3
Sulfur sludge	0	0.5	0.3	0	0	1.1	0.2	0
Land reclamation	0.4	0.3	0.4	0.6	0.4	0.3	0.4	0.6
Radiation	0.1	0.2	1.1	2.0	0.1	0.2	1.2	1.9
Onsite	–	–	0.1	0.1	–	–	0.1	0.1
Offsite	0.1	0.2	1.1	1.9	0.1	0.2	1.1	1.9
Total	14.5	44.0	60.3	127.8	12.3	30.2	43.9	87.2
Percentage of GNP	1.3	2.8	2.5	3.3	1.1	1.9	1.8	2.3

Note: Three dots (...) indicate that data are not available or are not separately reported. A dash (−) indicates that the amount is nil or negligible.

[a]Costs for 1975 are derived from the model and therefore may differ from actual costs.

FIGURE 1

Abatement resource costs as a percentage of GNP, assuming strict controls. Actual figures for 1971–75 are indicated by the lower line. Note: D (census series D) indicates population growth from 214 million in 1975 to 368 million by 2025. F (census series F) indicates population growth from 214 million in 1975 to 265 million by 2025. H (high) indicates GNP growth from $1,108 billion (1971 dollars) in 1975 to $6,212 billion in 2025. L (low) indicates GNP growth from $1,108 billion (1971 dollars) in 1975 to $3,859 billion in 2025.

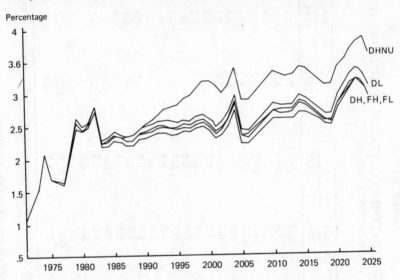

Second, while these percentages never become so large that they would be difficult to finance in the aggregate, their impact on individual sectors can be quite substantial. This can be seen in Figure 2 and Table 6, which assume that the standards specified in Table 1 will be met by certain dates and that capital for this purpose will be put in place over a four-year period prior to these dates.[3] If abate-

---

3. For example, the pattern shown by the chemical industry in Figure 2 is explainable in the following terms. The 1976 peak in expenditures occurs under strict standards because of efforts to apply conventional treatment standards; the 1982 peak happens when this sector moves from conventional treatment to advanced treatment technology standards on all equipment; and the expenditure increases starting in 1990 reflect replacement of earlier abatement investments plus the cost of converting to coal for process heat. Under relaxed enforcement, the 1976 peak is delayed until 1979; the 1982 peak is shifted to 1989, and it is smaller because only new plants are involved. The increases starting after 1990 also are delayed and smaller. These standards are compatible with environmental legislation up to but not after 1976. The large increase in abatement investments after 1990 results from the assumption that both the strict and relaxed standards will have to be upgraded over 1985 levels by 2000 and that this turn of the screw will be quite expensive.

FIGURE 2

Investments for selected industrial sectors, 1975–2000.
A, chemicals; B, steel; and C, electric utilities.

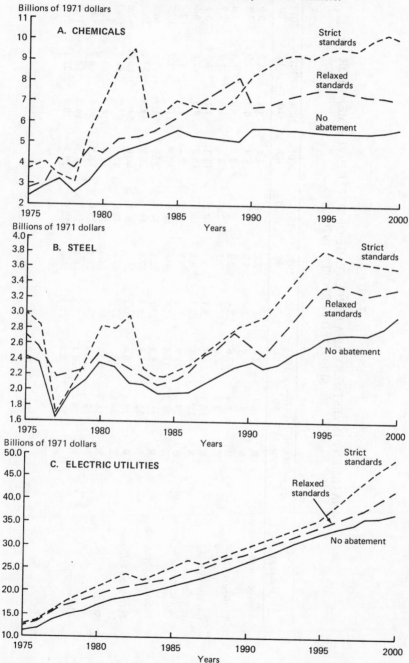

TABLE 6

ABATEMENT INVESTMENT AS A PERCENTAGE OF TOTAL INVESTMENT FOR
SELECTED PURPOSES, 1976–2025

Industry	Control standard[a]	1976–80	1981–85	1986–90	1991–95	1996–2000	2001–05	2006–10	2011–15	2016–20	2021–25
Average for the economy[b]	R	3.4	2.6	3.1	2.8	3.1	4.4	3.6	4.2	3.9	4.3
	S	4.8	4.9	3.7	4.7	5.9	5.9	6.5	7.9	7.3	8.1
Transportation[c]	R	1.4	2.6	2.4	2.3	2.2	2	1.9	1.8	1.8	1.8
	S	2.3	2.6	2.6	2.5	2.2	2	1.8	1.7	1.7	1.7
Electric utilities	R	10.7	9.3	8.1	5.4	8.2	13.3	7.1	6.3	5.6	5.4
	S	15	16.6	10.7	8.8	19.8	15.2	9.5	7.8	6.9	8.3
Municipal water treatment[d]	R	27	21.9	1.2	0.7	1.1	1.4	1.7	1.5	12	7.2
	S	34.8	27.4	11.6	10.6	10.8	10.9	11	21.7	17.7	10.8
Industrial chemicals	R	21	9.2	27.5	22.1	24.7	27.6	31.9	33.6	36.7	42.3
	S	31	33.9	26.4	37.8	44	38.9	49.3	57.1	56.1	56
Petroleum refining	R	24.9	8.4	20.2	35.8	26.9	80.8	51	60.6	47.4	50.6
	S	28.6	22	27	49.6	38.6	87	67.2	68.5	66.7	80.1
Steel	R	10.7	5.9	13	15.3	16	12.5	14.2	25	22.1	23.3
	S	12	16.8	14.7	27.4	24.6	18.5	30.4	46.3	40.1	40.3
Aluminum	R	9.4	4.4	7.5	11.2	20.9	16.7	14.2	14	18.4	15.6
	S	10.1	8.3	11.3	18.6	28.5	22.8	20.8	22.1	26.3	23.3

TABLE 6 (continued)

Industry	Control standard[a]	1976–80	1981–85	1986–90	1991–95	1996–2000	2001–05	2006–10	2011–15	2016–20	2021–25
Cement, concrete, and gypsum	R	14.7	4	12.4	14.1	15.5	17.8	17.5	30.6	31.7	28.7
	S	13.3	10.8	20.1	26.9	25.6	26.2	37.3	50.8	51.7	47.6
Paving plus asphalt	R	75.6	33	48.4	98.5	94	34	96.3	95	100	98.9
	S	78.6	49.3	65	99.1	95.8	49	98.6	97.6	100	99.6
Pulp mills	R	28.7	11.8	18.6	62.2	40.5	27.2	56.4	85.3	59.2	57
	S	28.1	19.5	41.2	81.5	54.8	46.8	82.6	92.8	73.7	75.4
Grain mill products	R	38.1	9.3	22.4	47.7	36.9	32.6	69.6	62	50.5	69.4
	S	39.5	23.4	30.9	60	47.7	49.6	85.1	78.2	71.5	85.5
Grain handling	R	9.4	2	14.9	10.4	10.1	14.7	7.4	26.6	14.9	20.8
	S	9.8	5.6	23.8	12.8	18.6	18.8	18.4	46.8	26	43

[a]R = relaxed pollution control standards; S = strict pollution control standards.

[b]Total abatement investment as percent of total investment in the economy.

[c]Total investment for this sector is the value of all transport equipment produced in the indicated period plus investment for abatement.

[d]Total investment for this sector is the expenditures on water treatment to meet the standards in force up to 1972 plus investment for controls above 1972 levels.

ment investments were added along with other investments in the normal course of expanding capacity, a less erratic and more manageable pattern of expenditures would have emerged. But the benefits to companies of delaying implementation as long as possible are so large that this outcome may be as unlikely in the future as it has been in the past. Indeed, given loopholes built into current legislation and judging from recent trends, we may observe substantially greater delays in implementing standards than those built into the relaxed case. To avoid this result, new ways would have to be found to force compliance and to help industries over these transition problems.

COMPARISON OF DAMAGE AND CONTROL COSTS

Our exclusive concern with control costs to this point is misleading. We ought to be concerned with *total* pollution costs, that is, pollution damage costs as well as pollution control costs. Figure 3 sums the two types of costs for different years and control policies. As can be seen, if environmental controls were kept at their 1975 level, pollution emissions and damage resulting from them would grow dramatically over time. If either the relaxed or strict policies were applied—both of which incorporate increasingly strict controls over time—control costs would increase rapidly, but damage costs would

FIGURE 3

Pollution control and damage costs for alternative environmental policies.

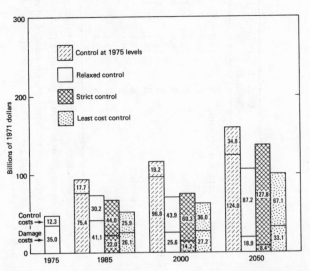

be reduced, with the result that total costs increase much more slowly. The principal difference between the relaxed and the strict standards during the first twenty-five years of the projection period is not in the total costs of pollution, but in the way these costs are allocated between damage costs on the one side and abatement or control costs on the other. The least-cost policy tends to have lower control costs in all years and higher damage costs in later years than does a relaxed policy because in no case does it allow for efforts to reduce risks by increasing controls beyond the point of minimum total cost.

Based on our assumed pattern of pollution control expenditures and damages, this diagram can be interpreted as indicating that it is better to opt for the strict policy during the first twenty-five years of the projection period and a relaxed policy thereafter. But it should be remembered that an additional benefit of more strict controls, which has not been quantified in monetary terms, is the reduced probability of instances where damage costs rise above the average or expected values incorporated into this figure. In other words, it might be worth some increase in total costs to avoid a small chance of very large environmental damages. An ethical question of how best to allow costs to occur is also involved; if total costs are nearly the same, we would prefer to spend more on controls to avoid more damages, since these often fall on third parties.

Another way in which to summarize the results of our simulation experiments is to construct a simple index of per capita welfare. We start with consumption per capita and subtract direct consumption expenditures for abatement and pollution damages per capita (see Table 7). The much larger portion of pollution control expenditures paid for directly by businesses has already been taken into account because these expenditures reduce the portion of output that can go to consumption. A least-cost pollution control policy would lead to the highest per capita welfare over time. A strict policy is, again, seen

TABLE 7

INDEXES OF PER CAPITA ECONOMIC WELFARE FOR
VARIOUS POLLUTION CONTROL POLICIES

Control policy	1975	1985	2000	2025
Relaxed controls	1.0	1.33	1.96	3.20
Strict controls	1.0	1.34	1.95	3.17
Least-cost controls	1.0	1.36	1.97	3.22
Controls at 1975 levels	1.0	1.30	1.91	3.14

to be better than a relaxed policy during the first twenty-five years of the projection period; thereafter, the relaxed policy has higher welfare levels. While these welfare indexes do not include values for risk reduction inherent in different policies and therefore understate the welfare value of the strict policy, our general conclusions are not affected by this omission.

FEEDBACK TO THE MACROECONOMY

Implicit in our procedure for entering investment requirements into our model (including investments to adjust to higher energy prices and investments for abating pollution) is the assumption that aggregate savings will increase to the extent necessary to finance this investment. This assumption may be unrealistic, at least for the decades of the 1980s and 1990s, when, according to our assumptions, the investment share of the GNP must remain above 21 percent. Since World War II, an investment rate (defined to include public construction and inventory accumulation) reaching 21 percent was achieved in only two years, 1950 and 1951.

If the investment rate cannot be increased to the required levels, the growth in labor productivity and hence in the GNP is likely to be less. A rough indication of the extent of the slowdown that might occur can be obtained by referring to other work of ours in which the private fixed investment rate was constrained to a maximum of 18 percent of the GNP.[4] Interpolation of those results indicates a reduction in GNP of between 4 and 12 percent starting in the mid-1980s when the additional energy and abatement investments are made to fit within an overall investment constraint of 18 percent of GNP. About one-fourth of the fall in GNP can be directly attributed to the investment requirements for pollution abatement.

These results suggest to us that in the end, the operation of the financial markets plus monetary and fiscal policy may be the most important factors in determining whether pollution control policy (along with adjustments to high energy prices) can be implemented without major disruptions. If fiscal and monetary policy mechanisms do not encourage savings to increase substantially and on a sustained basis over what they have been historically, the results could be serious.

---

4. Ridker, Watson & Shapanka, *Economic Energy and Environmental Consequences of Alternative Energy Regimes: An Application of the RFF/SEAS Modeling System,* in MODELING ENERGY-ECONOMIC INTERACTIONS: FIVE APPROACHES 135 (C. Hitch ed. 1977).

CONCLUSIONS AND QUALIFICATIONS

We have demonstrated that it is possible to simulate the long-term implications of environmental policy for the economy with an analysis that accounts for economic growth, increased population, and technical change. Under the assumed policies and assumed tides of economic and population growth, environmental damages resulting from the mass pollutants covered in this analysis are likely to remain the same or fall over time despite the growth in the economy and greater number of people at risk. Pollution control costs, though never a large percentage of GNP, will increase over time relative to both population and economic growth. The net effect is that total pollution costs (damage plus control costs) as a percentage of GNP or of consumption will decline slowly over time, and net economic welfare will increase. Thus, overall, the long-run impacts of pollution control on the national economy appear to be favorable given the assumptions of our analysis.

There are, however, a number of qualifying factors which should be kept in mind in judging this result. First, the policies we have analyzed are based on uniform national emission standards. In fact, some regions will be "overcontrolled," while others could experience deterioration in environmental quality; and some industries will find the costs of meeting regulations rising rapidly, while others will not be seriously burdened. Differential standards for special regions and some means of easing the transition for especially hard-hit sectors and regions would be worth serious consideration.

A related consideration stems from the fact that we have considered only aggregate packages of pollution control policies. If this analysis had been conducted in terms of individual pollutants, we would have found that the aggregate policies labeled "strict" and "relaxed" contain controls that are too strict for some pollutants and too lax for others.

Third, investments for pollution abatement and for energy-efficient capital (in response to high energy prices) may reduce macroeconomic growth if savings are not sufficient to finance these "extra" capital requirements. Some means of reducing national consumption and increasing savings will probably be necessary in the 1980s and 1990s to smooth the transition. This is, incidentally, a conclusion we could not have arrived at had our analysis been shorter term or less comprehensive.

Fourth, our analysis has focused mainly on mass pollutants at the national level. Other environmental problems may pose difficult choices in specific localities—for example, control of soil erosion, location of power plants, and land requirements for solid waste disposal and mining. Local constraints may increase costs by requiring remote siting or unusual protective measures. The cumulative effect of local decisions could be a significant reduction in the national economic growth rate.

Fifth, uncertainty about eventual environmental pressures may also result in slower economic growth. In some cases, one can point to only potential problems—acid rain, global warming from CO_2 buildup, difficulties in disposing of nuclear wastes, loss of topsoil—that are likely at some point to cause damages and possibly require costly adjustments. In still other cases—for instance, increasing population densities relative to resources in general but especially to land and water—the perception of growing environmental pressures may mean more regulations and conflicts, and the closing off of economic options.

To sum up, if the costs and damages we have assumed here are accurate, it appears that substantial control of the common mass pollutants can be achieved without undue interference with the national economy (and, in fact, can add to national economic welfare) as long as fiscal and monetary policy bring about some increase in savings and as long as hard-hit regions and sectors are helped. On the other hand, the picture for other environmental pressures is more worrisome. Our ignorance about some of these additional problems is profound. We frequently do not know what the environmental consequences of past human actions have been, let alone what present or future human behavior might bring. Nor do we know how long we may have to solve some problems before passing a possibly critical ecological threshold. For example, we do not seem to have reached the point today at which we need to restrict the use of some forms of energy, but we may not know until after the fact that we have reached that point. If less environmentally damaging forms of energy, for example, solar or fusion, come into use rapidly enough, we may never reach that point. By causing us to overreact or not react at all, our ignorance may make adjustments very costly. Had such costly adjustments due to ignorance been accounted for in our analysis, macroeconomic growth rates would probably be lower than we assumed at the outset.

APPENDIX

Estimates of national economic activity are derived using the national components of the Strategic Environmental Assessment System/Resources for the Future modeling systems (SEAS/RFF). This is a set of interlinked models, the core of which is a dynamic input-output model of the U.S. economy developed by Clopper Almon at the University of Maryland.[5] Its national economic accounting structure consists of 185 sectors delivering commodities to each other and to various final consumers (households, investors in fixed capital and inventories, government, and net exports). In addition, there are 364 side equations dealing with product and technology mixes within these sectors. The purpose of these side equations is to provide more detail for projecting pollution levels and abatement costs. All coefficients linking producing sectors with each other and with consumers are subject to change over time, some on the basis of econometrically fitted equations with time trends or lagged variables, but most on the basis of exogenously specified changes in technology, tastes, relative prices, supply constraints, and so on, determined on the basis of special studies.

In the case of technology, six main areas were emphasized: the substitution of concrete for lumber and steel in construction, increasing use of plastics and aluminum, improved efficiency of transportation equipment and the introduction of electric cars in significant numbers after 2000, process changes in primary metals production (which tend on net to improve efficiency and reduce pollutants), extensive development of communications and its partial substitution for some types of transportation, and energy supply and conversion technology.[6]

A submodel within this system estimates the investment and operating and maintenance costs associated with the control of pollution for 131 abating sectors. The costs calculated by the submodel for a given year create a demand for resources that is reflected through feedbacks which modify the output levels from the affected economic sectors. In turn, these changed output levels result in different sector growth rates from which the abatement costs are calculated during the next year.

National gross pollution levels for point sources (electric utilities, industry, residential and commercial fuel burning and process activities, and municipal sewage treatment) are calculated by applying gross pollution coefficients (units of gross pollution per unit of out-

---

5. C. ALMON, M. BUCKLER, L. HOROWITZ & T. REINBOLD, 1985: INTERINDUSTRY FORECASTS OF THE AMERICAN ECONOMY (1974).

6. Technical details, more complete discussion of all assumptions, and discussions of limitations are provided in R. RIDKER & W. WATSON, *supra* note 1; Ridker, Watson & Shapanka, *supra* note 4; A. Shapanka, Technological Assumptions and Their Use in Studying the Resource and Environmental Consequences of Population and Economic Growth in the United States (1977) (discussion paper, Resources for the Future, Washington, D.C.).

put) to output and side equation values. Net emissions are calculated as the product of gross emissions and the percent not controlled. These percentages correspond directly with the control levels and timing used in calculating abatement costs. These national point-source pollutants are assigned to regions using employment and population shares from government reports and special industry location studies.

In addition to the aforementioned point sources of pollutants, SEAS/RFF also calculates pollutants for transportation, urban run-off, mining, nonurban construction, forestry, and agriculture. Most of the estimates for these remaining categories—mainly nonpoint sources of pollution—are made at the regional level. In some cases, estimates of nonpoint pollutants are made initially at the national level and are then assigned to regions using appropriate shares.[7]

A three-step procedure is followed to develop our assumed pollution damage costs. Regional pollutants are transformed into ambient concentrations using dispersion models with appropriate transfer coefficients for each region; per capita average damages in dollars are calculated as a function of average per capita exposure; and per capita damages are multiplied by regional population and summed to obtain national damages for aggregated sources. National damage costs over a range of controls are obtained by changing assumed levels for national policy instruments.

Lying behind this procedure is a per capita regional pollution damage function that satisfies two properties. First, the regional damage function is concave upward with respect to exposure. The slopes or concavity of the function are determined by making them equal in a relative sense to the slopes of a few existing empirically estimated damage functions.[8] Second, the function assigns damages to regions so that for the year 1971, when per capita damages are multiplied by regional populations and summed, the result agrees with an exogenous national estimate for 1971 of total national pollution damages.[9] Satisfaction of these two properties is sufficient to determine a

7. Details of the calculations are provided in R. RIDKER & W. WATSON, *supra* note 1.

8. For example, if the empirical functions have slopes that increase by 50 percent as exposure goes from its median level to twice that amount, then the derived functions will also have the same relative change in slope over the same range of exposures relative to the median.

9. An estimate of national air pollution damages for 1971 ($20.2 billion in 1971 dollars) is taken from Gianessi, Peskin & Wolff, *The Distributional Implications of National Air Pollution Damage Estimates,* in THE DISTRIBUTION OF ECONOMIC WELL-BEING 201 (F. Juster ed. 1977). Estimated national water pollution damages for 1971 ($11.1 billion in 1971 dollars) are taken from H. HEINTZ, A. HERSHAFT & G. HORAK, NATIONAL DAMAGES OF AIR AND WATER POLLUTION (1976); Page, Harris & Epstein, *Drinking Water and Cancer Mortality in Louisiana,* 193 SCI. 55 (July 2, 1976).

unique regional per capita damage function that can be used to forecast damages.

Total regional damages are assigned to specific sources in proportion to each source's share in total exposures. In the case of water pollution, special assumptions are made to calculate the impact of sediment discharges by nonpoint sources. A weight for sediment from agriculture was selected so that in 1971 the damage model assigned $350 million of the $11.1 billion national water pollution damages to agricultural sediments. This weight was applied to sediment from other nonpoint sources and held constant for projection purposes.[10] The figure of $350 million was selected because it is roughly the middle of the range of damage estimates from agricultural sediment discharges reported by the best of the studies of this issue so far available.[11] That figure is only for damage associated with the silting of reservoirs and alteration of stream flows; it does not include any estimate for damage to water-based recreation activities. If a larger figure than $350 million had been used—which would have involved selecting a larger weight—less damage would have been assigned to point sources of water pollution, and the conclusions of our analysis could be affected.

In the case of air pollution, the analysis of least-cost controls covers all major sources and the major air pollutants. In contrast, the analysis of water pollution control determines least-cost controls only for electric utilities, industrial point sources, municipal wastewater treatment plants, and urban runoff sources. However, since damage costs depend upon emissions from all sources, assumptions had to be made about controls on the other sources.[12] These controls are kept constant as the model searches for least-cost controls for the indicated point and urban runoff sources.

---

10. This procedure was used only for deriving damage estimates for suspended and dissolved solids, the two pollutants associated most directly with sediment runoff. Other pollutants from nonpoint sources are treated exactly like pollutants from any other source; in effect, they are assigned a weight of one for entry into the damage model.

11. J. Wade & E. Heady, A National Model of Sediment and Water Quality: Various Impacts on American Agriculture (1976) (Report 67, Center for Agricultural and Rural Development, Iowa State University, Ames, Iowa).

12. For ore, coal, and minerals milling and mining, it is assumed that all facilities meet conventional treatment technology standards by 1980 and advanced treatment technology standards by 1985. The per unit sediment runoff from mining of ore, coal, and minerals is assumed to be reduced to about one half of its current level by 1985. Sediment runoff from nonurban construction (per unit of activity) is assumed to be one-half and one-fourth of current levels by 1985 and 2000, respectively. Acid mine drainage from abandoned coal mines is assumed to be one-half and one-fourth current levels by 1985 and 2000, respectively. Sediment runoff from agriculture on a per acre basis is assumed to be about two-thirds of its pre-1970 level, beginning in 1975.

Regulation and the Economy: Concluding Thoughts

HENRY M. PESKIN, PAUL R. PORTNEY, and ALLEN V. KNEESE

What conclusions can be drawn from the preceding papers? What should one bear in mind when thinking about environmental regulation and its effects on the economy? We believe there are at least five important observations to be drawn from this volume, several of which appear explicitly in one or more of the papers; others emerge from a consideration of the papers taken together.

First, it is a common and understandable failing for people to search for a single, simple cause of economic difficulties. For some, environmental and other regulation has become the "demon" upon which to pin the blame for high rates of inflation coupled with slow rates of economic growth. Understandable as this may be, it is wrong. Environmental regulation is but one of many factors contributing to the poor *measured* performance of the U.S. economy.

Consider for a moment the uncomfortably high recent inflation rate. While it is exacerbated by environmental regulation, as Portney's paper indicates, inflation is also influenced by a raft of other factors. These include, but are not limited to: deficits in the federal budget; the rate of growth of the money supply; the world oil cartel; fluctuations in domestic and world agricultural output; downward rigidity of wages and prices owing to the market power of employers and employees; changes in the skills of the work force and the saving habits of the population; tariffs, import quotas and other restrictions on foreign trade; and other factors, as well.

A similar multiplicity of causes can be identified to help explain sluggish economic growth, large numbers of unemployed, inadequate investment, foreign trade deficits and other economic difficulties. Hence, if the decade to come proves as trying as Bosworth suggests it may be, it will be important to keep in mind that no single cause, including environmental regulation, is likely to be responsible for more than a small part of the economic problems of the United States.

Second, it is necessary to develop a better understanding of measures of economic performance. We should not make a fetish of watching gross national product, the consumer price index, or productivity. Each of these measures is inadequate or, at the very least, open to misinterpretation, in some respect. For example, as Peskin

155

points out, the gross national product excludes many "outputs" which almost everyone would agree are important, including most of the benefits associated with clean air and water. Thus, GNP is not a particularly accurate measure of national well-being. Since labor productivity is, roughly speaking, GNP per worker, it, too, ignores the important nonmarketed outputs resulting from regulation. Hence, GNP and productivity will almost always be adversely affected by any policy, including regulation, that increases nonmarketed outputs at the expense of marketed ones. This will be true even when the trade-off between the two is quite favorable, that is, even when the clean air or water is worth the conventional output forgone to obtain them.

The consumer price index is open to similar misinterpretation. When the goods whose prices comprise the CPI become more expensive because of regulation, it is easy to believe that one is worse off. After all, is one not paying more for the same collection of goods? Not really. Along with the goods in the standard market basket, one also enjoys additional environmental quality following the implementation of environmental regulation. Thus, in one sense the size of the market basket has been expanded and the new environmental outputs must be weighed against the price and other adverse impacts of the regulations.

We are *not* suggesting that GNP, the CPI, or measures of productivity should be ignored. They are useful and important indicators of economic activity. Nevertheless, it is necessary to be aware of what these indicators can and cannot tell us by themselves. More information is needed to make intelligent decisions about environmental regulation than these indexes provide. At the head of the list are reliable estimates of the benefits of environmental policies. While the ability to estimate benefits is improving, there is still a sharp division of opinion as to the reliability of current estimates.

Third, the evidence reviewed here indicates that environmental regulation has a small but perceptible and generally adverse effect on price level, economic growth, productivity, international trade, and an ambiguous effect on employment. This comes through in Portney's review of the macroeconomic simulation studies, Haveman's and Christainsen's review of a variety of studies linking environmental regulation to productivity, Peskin's calculations of a "revised" GNP that better reflects environmental quality, and Ridker and Watson's longer run analysis of the impacts of regulation. Of course, others might refer to the effects identified in the papers in this volume as "large." Size is, of course, relative. What can be agreed upon, we believe, is that such effects may be important regardless of whether they are considered large or small.

Fourth, available measures may understate the total economic impacts of environmental regulation. This conclusion follows directly from the papers of Haveman and Christainsen, Portney, and Harrington and Krupnick. They all point to important respects in which environmental regulation can, among other things, create an uncertain milieu in which investment decisions must be made; discourage business growth or shunt it to second- or third-best locations; and increase the time required to begin projects. While all of these effects could prove to have important adverse economic implications, none can be readily identified using the analytical tools at hand. These indirect effects must be borne in mind when evaluating the pros and cons of regulation.

Fifth, even if one felt that environmental regulation was exerting only a small adverse effect on the economy, the search should continue for ways to reduce its cost where it can be done at little or no loss of environmental quality. For this reason, economists for years have been making a general case for the use of economic incentives in environmental policy. Harrington and Krupnick discuss several specific regulatory reforms intended to reduce the cost of maintaining the same level of environmental protection. Such reforms make sense at any time—why, after all, pay more for anything that can be had for less? Given the economic tenor of the times, however, such reforms may not only be sensible, but also essential if environmental protection is to be afforded increasing or even current levels of support. This conclusion may, in fact, be the most important message which these five papers impart.

Index